Order In The House

To: Brother George "God" man of God "my friend"

Arron D. Williams

Bookwell Publishing

Bookwell publishing

Contents - Order in the House

Acknowledgments

Foreword

Introduction

Authored by, Evang., Arron D. Williams

Acknowledgments :

First I give thanks to my precious Lord Jesus Christ, who picked me up out of the desolation of my horrid life to a lofty place in His presence to do His will for such a time as this.

I give thanks to my wife, Sher'ri, my daughter, Imani, and my cherished family members for sharing me with patience for the sake of the Body of Christ.

I also must thank my pastors Bishop Alfred A. and Co- pastor Susie C. Owens Jr. for their parental rearing of the ministry God has called me to fulfil before the world at large.

I thank my mother-in-law; Ingrid Johnson, Elder Sandra Jones, Dr. Barbra Reynolds, Deacon Shaun Johnson and any others not mentioned for their tireless help in various ways. I needed you all to accomplish this assignment for God's glory.

Finally, I would also like to thank Peter Crown (www.tucson-sunset.com), who provided the photograph on this book's cover.

Foreword:

In the first chapter and the fifth verse of Paul's letter to Titus, the apostle admonishes Titus that he had been left in Crete to "set in order the things that are wanting." In other words, he was saying to Titus that he was to bring organization to everything that was in disarray in the church. Paul understood that God is a God of order, and that promised move of God is contingent upon order existing in the Church.

God's mandate of order has in no way diminished over time, and He has raised up such men as Evangelist Arron D. Williams to declare: *"ORDER IN THE HOUSE!"* In this powerful message that elucidates God's original plan of order for Man, Evangelist Williams challenges the Church to come together, putting aside their differences, to implement God's plan for humanity. Evangelist Williams explains that God established order from the beginning of time and that it is the responsibility of the Church to demonstrate to the world God's order.

I pray that as you read the pages of this book, you would examine your own spiritual walk and allow the Spirit of God to conform you to His perfect will. Without a doubt, *__Order In The House__* is a God-inspired work that will walk you through the Word of God, illuminating not only God's plan for the Church, but for your life in particular.

Bishop Alfred A. Owens Jr., D. Min.
Senior Pastor
Greater Mt. Calvary Holy Church
Washington D.C.

Introduction

There is a still voice sometimes as small as a whisper and even a shout in the ears of the Church. It's not solely for the purpose of causing chill bumps to run down our spines. God wants us to really hear what He's saying to us by His Spirit. We must have an ear to hear this specific message God is revealing. It holds our purpose and direction for the next age looming around the corner.

God is certainly using a diverse multitude of men and women to declare this word to His Church. At this time in history, He has chosen to orchestrate a symphony of prophetic voices who are in concert to declare this message from God. The Church is waiting to move at the cue of their divine melody. It's imperative for us to be able to distinguish the voice of God, in spite of the noisome pestilence in the wind seeking to misguide us as we take the next step. Satan is well aware that if we miss our curtain call, the world will miss God's stellar performance through His star vessel, the Church. Lives hang in the balance, caught between hell's fire and heaven's haven. We must respond to God's call to us to serve . Do you hear Him!

I feel like praying: "God help your people to hear what you are saying to them right now! Don't allow us, dear God, to continue to be deceived by that devil. Sharpen our sense of hearing so we can tune into your word. Direct us, Father, to be able to do your will. Cause us, Lord, to be whom you have ordained us to be from the beginning of time, and help us to come to the fulness of knowledge and maturity in Christ our Savior and Lord . In Jesus' Name I pray, amen! I believe if you pray with me brothers and sisters this will come to pass.

I have the awesome task of declaring a word of inspiration unto the Church. My voice is mingled with many others who are more qualified by virtue of their status in the Church hall of fame, faith and power. I am in awe of them, since they tower over me. Nevertheless, I must speak according to my charge from God. I don't want to end up like Jonah in the belly of a prepared fish because of my disobedience.

He has called me to sound a trumpet in the ears of the Church as a clarion call unto order. We have been *out of order*. God wants us to get to the level He wants us to be at during this present age. The previous generation has passed to us the responsibility of carrying a baton that must light up this dark era. A harvest of souls awaits us.

We must de-emphasize the things that have preoccupied our valuable time. Shake off the garment of slothfulness and wipe the sleep out of your sluggish eyes. We must hear the alarm being sounded that commands us, *get in order*. Church, arise!

Ride with me now on the wave of faith to the shore of our intended destiny, so we can be the people God has predestined before the beginning of time. This isn't being said for my health. I am speaking to you so that your ears will hear what the Spirit of the Lord is saying unto the Church.

Chapter 1.- We Need Order

In the midst of this chaos-filled world there's a moral degeneracy taking place and for this reason people are calling what is right wrong and what is wrong right. It's not hid under any cloak of deception, but it is openly being exhibited before our very eyes. There is a lack of adhesiveness and consistency to keep things properly together in the world around us. Due to this sad situation all of humanity seems to be in pursuit of something or someone to stabilize them from this tragic state. This has created an atmosphere where in many dictators, political leaders, religious opportunist and governments are arising, trying to lead the lost citizens of society. Sadly their feeble attempts have yielded no good results and the disorder continues with an accelerated downward spiral.

Since they can't offer true direction; who or from where, can we find real order? Who will stand up and disperse the crowd of imposters? Who will rise to rescue the world, a damsel in distress? Prince of peace and King of kings, come for the world needs you right now.

A.   **The Order of God -**

I Corinthians 14:33, *"For God is not the author of confusion, but of peace, as in all churches of the saints."*

He looked from the distance seeing her in the sunlit valley. He came closer hearing the voice of her distress cry out for help. In haste He rushed to her place of calamities. It was only He that could save her from chaos. Reaching in a valiant attempt to prevent her from falling, He caught this lady before she hit the ground. He is a savior, a prince; no, a king or all of the above. No matter, the day is redeemed and nothing is lost. Jesus has arisen to meet the Church's need.

God has established order in creation. It is subjected to what He has prescribed and it harmonizes with what He has predestined. From the beginning, God crafted His handy works with the intent of bringing forward a concerted parade of beauty. Therefore, we can conclude that He never authored anything with the intent of causing confusion, but we must recognize He is the God of order.

1.   **In the Beginning -**

Genesis 1:1-31 *"In the beginning God created the heaven and the earth.2, And the earth was without form, and void; And darkness was upon the face of the deep. And the Spirit of God moved upon the face of the waters. 3. And God said, Let there be light: there was light. 4. And God saw the light, that it was good: And God divided the light from darkness. 5. And God called the light Day, and the darkness Night. And the evening and the morning were the first day. 6. And God said, Let there be a firmament in the midst of the waters, and let it divide the waters from the waters. 7. And God* made the firmament, and divided the waters which were under the firmament from the waters which were above the firmament: and it was so. 8. And God called the firmament Heaven. And the evening and the morning were the second day. 9. And God said, Let the waters under the heaven be gathered together unto one place, and let the dry land appear: and it was so. 10. And God called the dry land Earth; and the gathering together the waters called them Seas: and God saw it was good. 11. And God said, Let the earth bring forth grass, the herb yielding seed, and the fruit tree yielding fruit after his kind, whose seed is in itself, upon the earth :and it was so. 12. And the earth brought forth grass, and herb yielding seed after its kind, and the tree yielding fruit, after his kind: and God saw it was good. 13. And the evening and the morning were the third day.14. And God said, Let there be lights in the firmament of the heaven to divide the day from the night; and let them be for signs, and for seasons, and for days, and years: 15. And let them be for lights in the firmament of the heaven to give light upon the earth. 16. And God made two great lights; the greater light to rule the day, and the lesser light to rule the night: He made the stars also. 17. And God set them in the firmament of heaven to give light upon the earth, 18. And to rule over the day and over the, and to divide the light from the darkness: and God saw that it was good. 19. And the evening and the morning were the fourth day. 20. And God said, Let the waters bring forth abundantly the moving creature that hath life, and the fowl that may fly above the earth in open firmament of heaven. 21. And God created great whales, and every living creature the moveth, which the waters brought forth abundantly, after their kind, and every winged fowl after its kind: god saw that it was good. 22. And God blessed them, saying, be fruitful and multiply, and fill the waters in the seas, and let fowl multiply in the earth. 23. And the evening and the morning were the fifth day. 24. And God said, Let the *earth bring forth the living creature after his kind, cattle, and creeping thing, and beast of the earth after his kind: and it was so. 25. And god made the beast of the earth after his kind and cattle after their kind, and every thing that creepeth upon the earth after his kind: and God saw that it was good. 26. And God said, Let us make man in our own image, after our likeness: and let them have dominion over the fish of the sea, and the fowl of the air, and over the cattle, and over the earth and over every creeping thing that creepeth upon the earth. 27. So God created man in His own image, in the image of God created He him; male and female created He them. 28. And God blessed them, and God said unto them, be fruitful, and multiply, and replenish the earth, and subdue it: and have dominion over the fish of the sea, and over the fowl of the air, and over every living thing that moveth upon the earth. 29. And God said, Behold, I have given you every herb bearing seed, which is upon the face of all the earth, and every tree, in the which is the fruit of the tree yielding seed; to you it shall be for meat. 30. And to every beast of the earth , and to every fowl of the air, and to every thing that creepeth upon the earth, wherein there is life, I have given every green herb for meat:and it was so. 31. And God saw every thing that He have made, and, behold, it was very good and the evening and the morning were the sixth day."*

When God created the earth, He not only created it in an orderly fashion, but He also subjected it and all in it to the same order. If we follow the text above, we will see the great care God took to chronologically create all He created.   He employed His righteous judgement and holy expertise as He decisively lined up His creative itinerary.

The earth and the waters were the most basic among His creations;

Then light and darkness was designated to distinguish day from night. Water was then separated by the emerging earth that formed the land for other habitation. Herbs and trees came forth brilliantly with wonderful colors as their foliage unfolded. The light, soil and water they needed to exist had already preceded them. Cattle, fowl, and every creeping creature upon the earth were next to follow and everything they needed preceded them. Finally man, both male and female, was created in their splendor and excellence. The depth of calculation God had when He created all in creation, blows our minds, as we review how He provided everything man needed to maintain their life, vocation, and relationship with their God.

Man was the last of God's creation; He saved the best for last, a sort of grand finale to close a chapter which would begin a long episode called humanity. Man was the most complex of all of His creations. It was man alone that had God consciousness, for he walked and talked with God in the cool of the day. Yet, he also was subjected to the order of God despite his relationship with God. Although he worked within the confines of predisposed order, it was the Lord's gift to him {them} to choose. Contrary to what some might reason, the freewill of man did not conflict with the sovereignty of God, for it was God's choice to give it to him. Moreover, order was made for man and not man for order. He was given the means of operating within and yet he could choose to be outside of order. This allowed man, of his own volition to serve God. Thus, man's love for God could truly be tested. God wanted man to love Him just as He did him.

When God designed everything with and in order, it wasn't an after thought. He intended that everything should be in order from the very beginning. Speaking into what was nothing, God out of the creativity of His thoughts, took the paintbrush of His words and painted the beauty of the world across the canvas of what was something from what was nothing. He said with godly artistry "Let there be," and it was so. The words being completely at His command refused to deny the Master Artist His gallery of works. As a matter of fact, they hastened to accomplish His every thought. Letters, words, phrases, sentences, paragraphs and an entire discourse banded together in concert to do what God wanted. The word of God then became the framework of all existence, upon these declarations from God hinged all tangible things. What's so awesome about this is God became so engrossed in His own work that He became *the word* which carved everything which was made. Then He decided to do a self portrait and He projected it perfectly in man. With the clay of the earth He made him in His own likeness and image.

The Apostle John eloquently declares, *"the Word was God; The Word became flesh and dwelt among us."* This Word is Jesus Christ, the visible image of the invisible God, who thought it not robbery to be equal with Him. When the text in Genesis reflects that *"God said,"* we know the word was indeed on the scene being one with Him. The Holy Ghost is described, also as having moved upon the face of the earth when it was void and without form. All who are in the trinity are participating in creation. We again see the evidence of this in agreement when the Bible says "Let us make man in our own image."

I'll leave the battle of the theology to the scholars and critics. My only point is that God did all in order and is a God of Order.

a.   **Creation Relates to Humanity -**

Not only do we read how God is connected in the Godhead in

creation, but we also see a relationship between the things that were created. We can follow the order by precedence from the crown of creation, man, or down to the less superior things like animals, plants and the elements (water, the earth, stars, sun, moon and heavens). The basis of this link is established in the text of Genesis 1:26. It is here that we see that God by giving man dominion over the other forms of creation, caused an unbreakable band to form by His intentional design.

Romans 8:18-22- *"For I reckon that the sufferings of this present time are not worthy to be compared with the glory that is to be revealed in us.19. For the earnest expectation of the creature waiteth for the manifestation of the sons of God 20. For the creature was made subject to vanity, not willingly, but by reason of him who hath subjected the same in hope. 21. Because we creature itself also shall be delivered from bondage of corruption into the glorious liberty of the children of God. For we know the whole creation groineth and travaileth until now."*

We read in this above text how this band will persist until the day man's redemption is finalized. Creation is subjected to man's penalty and is also freed by humanities' ultimate deliverance. This refers to when the lamb and the lion will lie down together that the peace that the righteous experience will also be their victory.

To further show this relationship, we read in the Old testament how animals and plants became a vehicle of sacrifice for man's transgressions against God. They laid their lives, without choice, on the line in order that man could temporarily be forgiven for his state of sinfulness. Another connection between man and creation is seen when a donkey carries the Lord to be the redemption of man. I can imagine its delight to partake in what would mean his and other animal's freedom. The bottom line is that there is a common thread woven through humanity and creation, binding them together. This relationship between creation and man only speaks further to the intricate order with which God has been consistent throughout Bible history. This consistency continues and will do so even in eternity.

As we look at the order in man's relationship to creation, we cannot avoid acknowledging the disorder. It's evident that we don't have dominion over creation at present. The results of this disorder has caused numerous catastrophes to occur in nature and also, many animals are attacking man beyond his control. Plants meant for the benefit of man, are now used to destroy them through chemical warfare, inner city warfare, and urban warfare. Drugs are being sold everyday, leaving many addicted to them. Hope only rests in the redemption of the righteous. It's only through God's elect that the world will see any true order. The order that exists now isn't order at all. It's a patched up, quick fix, and fairy tale order established by men.

Please come where I am trying to take you Church while we attempt to unravel the tangled and mangled order of the world in our next discussion.

B.   **The Order of the World -**

Psalm 14:1, *"The fool hath said in his heart, There is no God. They are corrupt, they have done abominable works, there is none that doeth good."*

While evaluating the world's order over a period of time, we can access the record. The Bible and many other historical manuscripts have documented that disorder is borne out of the initial confusion in the Garden of Eden. What I find weird about this obvious disorder is that the very people that are trapped in its maze appear to prefer society in this condition. But, of course, we know that if this gospel is hid, it is because the god of this world, Satan, has blinded their minds so that they won't believe in the truth. The order they have declared as order is false and will ultimately be exposed for what it really is, **disorder.**

For a few minutes let's acknowledge and then reverence the Lord for having complete and total control. For He is sovereign and the author and finisher of our faith, the One who constructs all that is established in creation. *"Except the Lord build the house, the laborers build in vain that build it;"* And again, *"not by power not by might, but by my Spirit saith the Lord of hosts."*

Well, this state has deceived many into thinking they are self-sufficient. The truth is made known in the text which says, *if someone says there is no God (or order of God), they are fools (one not truly knowledgeable)-(paraphrased).* This scripture may seem harsh in denouncing the one who doesn't believe in God by calling them a fool; but if we really think about it, it is ridiculous to think we can exist without our Creator. It's like a baby who, being born of his or her parents, one day grows up after being nurtured by them suddenly decides to say these aren't my parents or, moreover, I just appeared without the need of a man or a woman as a means of my birth.

The world has estranged itself from God the Father in such a way that they have tried to please themselves. This has been done through words and deeds that say; "There is no God."

What people rather have done, is to exalt such televised characters in the persons of animals, elements of the earth, and super human figures. And further they have sought the strength or help they purport they can get from them. They by doing this are denying God as being God. Only He can provide all of humanities needs. In addition to exalting cartoon characters and media personalities as gods, the world has tried through medical and science to rebuild man. Cloning and genetic altering have been our latest ventures. Again I say that only God can fix what is broken, for He is our heavenly Father.

1.   <u>Nimrod's Government</u> -

Genesis 11;1-9 *"And the whole earth was of one language, and of one speech. 2. And it came to pass, as they journeyed from the east, that they found a plain in the land of Shinar; and they dwelt there. 3. And they said one to another, Go to let us make brick, and burn them thoroughly. And they had brick for stone, and slime had they for mortar. And they said, Go to , <u>let us build us a city and a tower, whose top may reach unto heaven;and let us make us a name, lest we be scattered</u> abroad upon the face of the whole earth. 5. And the Lord came down to see the city and the tower, which the children of men builded. 6. And the Lord said, Behold, the is one, and they have all one language; and this they began to do: and now nothing will be restrained from them, which they have imaged to do. 7. Go to, let us go down, and there confound their language, that they may not understand one another's speech. 8. So the Lord scattered them abroad from thence upon the face of all the earth; and they left off to build the city. 9. Therefor the name of it is called Babel; because the Lord did there confound the language of all the earth and from thence did the Lord scatter them abroad upon the face of all the earth."*

In this above text, the featured character is one of the most renowned world leaders recorded in any historical manuscript. Nimrod, as he is called, accomplished probably what is one of the most sought after political achievements in all of leadership since the beginning of time. He was able to get people together, which is one of the hardest things to do and we could go further to say it is almost impossible. But this world leader was able to do this because he had some valuable advantages. The people were of one mind, language and purpose.

The same concept exists as we talk about the societies throughout the world. Yet the basis of their agenda has become the very hindrance to their intended success. The flaw is that they seek to make themselves a name, and it has tainted their purity of purpose. The world carries the spirit of Nimrod's government and has sought to fulfill their own agenda and it has not included God. Nimrod government's goal was to fulfil their selfish ambitions. The governments of this world have done the same. Yeah, you may hear various people saying, "I have faith", but they never address in whom they have faith. This is because their faith is in self or someone or something who isn't God Most High. The idea which develops as a result of this mentality is a "do it yourself" or "I can do it through me" mind-set. This is the plight of the Nimrod styled government. It abases God for who He is and exalts man for who he is not. But God, of course, will never allow any fleshy agenda or self-promoted glory to stay in His presence. God's glory is the one thing you don't want to try to steal. To do so will mean destruction.

This brings to mind a story in the Old Testament that is related to this conversation of stealing God's glory.

I Sam. 5:1-5 *"And the Philistines took the ark of God, and brought it from Eb'-en-e'-zer unto Ash'-dod. 2. When the Philitines took the ark of God, they brought it into the house of Da'-gon, and set it by Dagon. 3. And when they of Ashdod arose early in the morrow, behold, Dagon was fallen upon the face to the earth before the ark of the Lord. And they took Dagon, and ste him in his place again. 4. And when they arose early on the morrow morning, behold Dagon was fallen upon his face to the ground before the ark of the Lord; and the head of Dagon and both the palms of his hands were cut off upon the threshold; only the stump of Dagon was left to him."*

The Ark of the Covenant had been stolen from the people of Israel and ended up in the custody of the Philistine nation who stole it. They placed this sacred furniture in the presence of Dagon, who they worshiped as the all supreme god. God refused to be thought of as less in the presence of this false god, so He knocked it down both times that the Philistines put it back upright. However, since the Philistines continued to exalt this imitation, the third time He caused Dagon to fall and shatter into pieces with its head being left decapitated where it fell. God doesn't play with His glory.

I must address this Nimrod spirit that has found a place within our own government system. It is lurking within the halls of such esteemed places as the White House, the House of Representatives, and the United States Senate. God gave me a revelation some years ago while I was taking my daily walk from the Monument along the mall area in Washington, D.C.. God began to trouble my spirit about this nation as I approached the Capitol building. It was there that I began to look at it when God began to say to me how men had built this government in pursuit of a type of utopia. He went on to say how He had nothing to do with establishing it. Finally, He demonstrated to me the parallel between the Nimrod type of government and this one. Finally the last words were, no nation can remain intact except their steps are ordered by God.

Psalm 33:12 *"Blessed is the nation whose God is the Lord; and the people whom He hath chosen for His own inheritance."* Matthew 7:24-17- *"Therefore whosoever heareth these sayings of mine, and doeth them, I will liken him unto a wise man, which built his house upon a rock: 25. And the rain descended, and the floods came , and the winds blew, and beat upon the house; and it fell not: for it was founded upon a rock. 26 and every one that hear these sayings of mine, and doeth them not, shall be liken unto a foolish man, which built his house upon sand:27. And the rain descended, and the floods came, and the winds blew, and beat upon the house; and it fell: and great was the fall."*

The Word is the foundation of any stable dwelling. Not just the book, but the actual living of the contents of the Holy Bible. Political jargon we often hear being said in campaign speeches, aren't a true example of God's foundation. Only the Word of God is meant to provide people and their nations with this kind of stability. And it is unlike the false sense of religion being perpetuated out of the mouths of this nation's public officials, who use statements like "God bless America," or "I am praying for our nation." We know this is true because the evidence of their double-talk comes back to haunt them when their misdeeds are exposed for what they are. At one side of their mouth they promote moral values and God, while out of the other side they declare, "Blacks ought to be glad they have opportunities and should forget the past because everything is equal now.", "There is no need for affirmative action or forty acres and a mule." The last time I checked God's Word, it declared in Psalm 62:10 *"Trust not in oppression, and become not vain in robbery: if riches increase, set not your heart upon them."* People are not to trust in oppression as if it's okay to put somebody down for any reason, including their color. Well, anyway, God wants to overthrow the lie and unmask the facade of our nation. It is only then that we can face it enough to allow God to fix it. Our self-constructed tower which seeks a utopia of a self-fulfillment must fall. Politicians must stop telling this lie to this nation's citizens. Yes, I do believe there are people who are under God in our nation and the world. I am not disputing that fact. And they are of all colors and classes. But our leaders and general populace alike in this country and abroad must walk more circumspectly to the word of God.

a.   **What Nation is really under God?**

Proverbs 14:34 *"Righteousness exalts a nation, But sin is a reproach to any people."*

As was said earlier, we must note the lack of integrity within our ranks by placing the spotlight on unresolved and sinful issues. Abort this politically-correct platform designed to avoid the real issue; wrong is wrong and right is right. We need to call sin out for what it is in our nation and stop making excuses for the hatred we harbor, the racism we ignore, and the host of other lies we pacify daily. Patriotism has overshadowed the truth and obscured the facts. We need a true relationship with God. There is a false sense of security when we sing our national songs in harmony across each state. Therefore, we as a whole have felt no desperate need to run to God, because our nation has been elevated to be worshiped as a supreme and sovereign god.

Years ago, Martha Washington stitched together this nation's flag, so it could be flown over its hills and valleys. A new generation of

Americans have risen also sowing a tapestry that is meant to cover what only God Most High through Jesus' blood can cover. To say we are a nation under God must mean more than just a few lyrics sung to a nationally-recognized tune. To carry such a banner that is magnificently colored with these words means, our nation allows God to set its standards. And if it should stray from these standards, it will cry out for the righteousness of their God, wailing and weeping for repentance.

II Chronicles 7;14 , *"If my people , who are called by my name , shall humble themselves , and pray, seek my face, and turn from their wicked ways ;then will I hear from heaven, and will forgive their sin, and will heal their land."*

Only if our great nation would really get under God and yield its will to Him who is the one and only God, Jesus Christ, then we can be the greater nation. It may mean putting away racism, sexual improprieties, hatred, materialism, and all things that hinder us from having a relationship with God. But if we continue to be a nation that stands for nothing, we will easily persist to fall for everything. Who will stand today as you read the words written here? Is there anyone among us that will rise up to be counted? I warn you that you most certainly won't win any popularity contests or even get nominated to have your name put in the world's light of fame. But stand up anyway!

I may sound excited, but its because an uprising like this will cause an explosive revival to break out in our nation. Just thinking about it causes me to begin to hear the multitudes crying out throughout the hollow valleys and mountain sides across our country, as I write. Do you hear their emotionally overwhelmed voices? They are calling out to the God of heaven and of earth. He is calling such a multitude to seek His kingdom and His righteousness. This is the hour to be revived.

1. **CPR = Revival**

People are looking for something or someone to resuscitate them in every area of their lives. The only problem is that they have the wrong savior and the wrong means of revival. The world has gone after drugs, dictators, movie stars, musical artists, and other gods. The list goes on, but none of these can revive man to his rightful state. They only offer a temporal high that will eventually come crashing down to reality. If the truth is told, only C-hrist's P-ower and R-esurrection can save the destitute and the deprived of this incapacitated society we live in. The world is in a comatose state of being; and is existing solely by means of life-support. God is keeping the world alive although they are not responsive to His mercy. People who are in a coma don't move, eat on their own, or do anything to make us know they are alive. As a matter of fact, if a monitor didn't tell us they were alive we would assume they were dead. From a spiritual perspective, it's like being unconscious of the spirit meant to allow us to commune with God. Man in this state can't hear from God or respond to God. Any word of direction is null and void due to his or her inability to perceive the things and voice of God. If humanity will be revived, it will be by a spiritual CPR. Jesus is the means of that renewal of life in us.

Once in the gospels He breathed on His disciples giving them an introductory portion of life called the Holy Ghost. It was, the absence of God's Spirit in the first place that caused the decaying effects to take its course. The scriptures said, *"my Spirit will not always strive with man."* So it is the Spirit that quickens. Jesus wants to breath life into the defiled spirits of humanity to revive them with His Spirit.

Prayer; Lord, I pray, right now that you revive men and women with your resurrection power. Open blind eyes and cause the hearts of men to seek after you. Help us, dear God, to sense your presence and power in this world. Come now, Father, in the fullness of your strength to save and breathe on nations worldwide. In Jesus' Name, I pray, Amen.

2.   **Upon Christ's Shoulders** -

Isaiah 9:6-7: *"For unto us a child is born, unto us a Son is given and the government will be upon His shoulder and His name will be called Wonderful, Counselor, Mighty God, Everlasting Father, Prince of Peace. Of the increase of His government and peace there will be no end. Upon the throne of David and over His kingdom to order it and establish it with judgment and justice. From that time forward, even forever, the zeal of the Lord of hosts will perform this."*

Up until now we have discussed such things as the need for order, the order of God, and the order of the world with more defining sub-topics included. Now we are entering a corridor to discuss the foundation and cornerstone upon which all stands in order to be established forever. Looking back, the Bible testifies about this from Genesis to the end of the Bible. We see numerous historical accounts that flow from earlier years to this present day.

John 1:3 - *"All things were made through Him, and without Him nothing was made that was made"*. Hebrews 1:2 - *"God, who at various times and in various ways spoke in time past to the Fathers by the prophets, 2. has in these last days spoken to us by His Son, whom He has appointed heir of all things, through whom also he made the world."* Ephesians 2:20 - *"Having been built on the foundation of the apostles and prophets, <u>Jesus Christ, Himself, being the chief cornerstone.</u>"*

We could go on all day quoting scripture references, but you can do a deeper study in your private devotion. For now let's take government as a topic in particular. Relating to our original text, Isaiah 9:6-7, where it prophetically declared that the government shall be upon His shoulder—meaning Jesus Christ, know That this has not yet completely taken place. The Church is setting the tone for this to happen. God has predestined this to take place. When it does, it will mean Christ ruling all of the nations with an iron rod and with complete and sovereign power.

Since we are priming the world atmosphere for Jesus' soon return, we then must better understand the role of the Church in getting in order to do God's predestined will for this present day.

C.   **The Order of the Church -**

I Peter 2:9-10 (C) *"But you are a chosen generation, a royal priesthood, a holy nation, His own special people, that you may proclaim the praises of Him who once were not a people of God, who had not obtained mercy, but now have obtained mercy."*

God has so ordained that by the conduit of Jesus Christ His people should come forth from the womb of divine destiny to accomplish what has been hid from the beginning; before the earthly walk of Jesus, our Lord.

It's time now to get into one of the best parts of the book. This portion from here on out deals with the central reason for the book. God has called His people, the Church, to do greater works than He did; greater exploits in the earth, and the prerequisite will require us to get in the order to which God is calling us.

1.   **The Pattern of the Temple -**

Take for example the pattern of the temple, we can gather from it how the course of order should be. It is a shadow of order that can be used to reestablish God's order in the Church.

Exodus 25:8-9, 40 (NKJV) "*8. And let them make me a sanctuary that I may dwell among them, 9. According to all that I show you that is the pattern of the tabernacle and the pattern of all its furnishings, just so shall you make it. - 40. And see to it that you make them according to the pattern which was shown you on the mountain.*" Hebrews 9:1-11, *"Then verily the first covenant had also ordinances of divine service, and a worldly sanctuary. 2. For there was a tabernacle made; the first wherein was the candlestick, and the table, and the shew bread; which is called the sanctuary. 3. And after the second veil, the tabernacle which is called the Holiest of holies. 4. Which had the golden censer, and the ark of the covenant overlaid round about with gold, wherein was the golden pot that had manna, and Aaron's rod that budded, and the tables of the covenant; 5. And over it the cherubims of glory shadowing the mercy seat ; of which we cannot now speak particularly. 6. Now when these things were thus ordained, the priests went always into the first tabernacle, accomplishing the service of God. 7. But into the second went the high priest alone once every year, notwithout blood, which he offered for himself, and for the errors of the people: 8. The Holy Ghost this signifying, that the way into the holiest was not yet made manifest, while as the first tabernacle was yet standing; 9. Which was a figure for the time then present, in which were offered both gifts and sacrifices, that could not make him that did the service perfect, as pertaining to the conscience; 10. Which stood only in meats and drinks, and divers washings, and carnal ordinances, imposed on them until the time of reformation. 11. But Christ being come a High Priest of good things to come, by a greater and more perfect tabernacle, not made with hands, that is to say, not of this building;"*

We must pay close attention to the pattern of the temple, since we are referred to as the temple of the Holy Ghost in scripture. It is acceptable to compare how the temple shown to Moses in the mount was established in order as the Church should be in order. The Hebrew's text states that there is a heavenly pattern being manifested in the earth realm. If Moses went to the mountain to get what it was God had for him to build, we also must go higher before our sweet Savior to get the plans for what it is God is calling us to do. This would mandate an old-fashioned revival. We need to take a sabbatical toward God, away from all distractions. If we will get in order, we must get His plan for order. Even if it means climbing rough mountain sides overlooking nauseating cliffs and intimidating ledges. We must lay-out, not in any specific location, but together we must elevate our hearts and minds to the lofty places of heaven to get the plans to conquer hell.

There's no other way to ascend to a spiritual utopia other than to pray and to worship God most high. It's then we can get above flesh and get into the presence of the Father. Help us, Lord Jesus, right now.

So the Church is a present-day example of the temple built by Israel for the presence of God to dwell in. Let's look at the construction of the temple and the meanings behind the actual building and its furnishings, to compare this pattern with the pattern God is calling us to adopt today.

First, we must note that God called the people involved with the temple out from where they were in Egyptian bondage to a place of peace and promise in Canaan. This illustrates to us that God sought to have a relationship with these people. And to further consummate this union, God showed them what would hinder their relationship, sin. In pointing out sin to them, He also showed Israel the vehicle by which they could be reconciled to Him, in spite of sin's blemish. Thus, God spoke to Moses giving him the means of their unification with Him, the temple.

Before this the ten commandments were given to expose sin and how it offended God, along with numerous other ordinances and laws. God further indicated to Moses how to repent of these sins while Israel was leaving Egypt.

Exodus 20:24, *"An altar of the earth thou shalt make unto me, and shalt sacrifice thereon thy burnt offerings, and thy peace offerings, thy sheep, and thine oxen: in all places where I record my name I will come unto thee, and I will bless thee."*

The altar gave them a means to commune with God by praying and sacrificing until the temple was built. Indeed we must pray with a sacrificial heart. For this is our primary means of uniting ourselves with God. Soon after the altar was made, the temples' construction began. This was a better means of reconciling man with God. It provided a place where God could come to man and demonstrate His mercy, grace, and power.

God continues to speak to Moses about the pattern of the temple and all its sacred contents. He even reveals the smallest details and who the people are who He has anointed to build it.

Before we finish this segment of our discussion, we must also note that the temple is a shadow of how God will sanctify, consecrate, anoint and use His vessels for a specific purpose. He also does this for all of us who are in the Body of Christ. The shadow shows us that Jesus is the temple structure itself and we are the vessels in Christ. The furniture in the tabernacle, (the number of man)six major pieces in all, had separate yet common purposes to fulfill for the glory of the Lord.

1)   The alter of burnt offering

2)   The bronze laver

3)   The table of shew bread

4)   The gold lamp stand

5)   The altar of incense

6)   The Ark of the Covenant

The anointing oil was the (number of completion)seventh thing which sealed, sanctified and consecrated these instruments of service before God. These instruments were meant to bring man together with God and, yet, maintain the priest that would be set aside for the service of the Lord in uniting man to God. Alone, the vessels would only be useless pieces of wood and valued metal without the most valuable ingredient. The anointing oil that sanctified these sacred objects was also the means which enabled them to act as God's means of expressing His mercy.

The parallel that the shadow conveys to us is that God wants to use us as a body of believers by enabling us through His Spirit, who is represented in the temple by the oil. Like Jesus, the temple was anointed so we who are in Christ can be recipients of His anointing that He left to comfort us and empower us to minister to the world.

2.   **Pentecost Re-Establishes Order -**

Acts 2:1-18 *"And when the day of Pentecost was fully come, they were all with one accord in one place. 2. And suddenly there came a sound as of a rushing mighty wind, and it filled all of the house where they were sitting. 3. And there appeared unto them cloven tongues like as of fire, and it sat upon each of them. 4. And they were filled with the Holy Ghost, and began to speak with other tongues , as the Spirit gave them utterance. 5. And there was a dwelling at Jerusalem Jews, devout men, out of every nation under heaven.6. now when this was noised abroad, the multitude came together, and were confounded, because that every man heard them speak in his own language. 7. And they were all amazed and marvelled, saying one to another, Behold, are not these which speak Galileans? 8. And how hear we every man in our own language, wherein we were born? 9. Parthianns, and Medes, and Elamites, and the dwellers inn the mesopotamiaa, aaand in Judea and Cappadadocia, in Pontus and Asia, 10. Phrygia, and in the parts of Libya about Cyrene, and strangers of Rome , Jews and proselytes, 11. Cretes and Arabians, we do hear them speak in our own tongues the wonderful works of God. 12. And they were all amazed, and were in doubt, saying one to the other, What meaneth this? 13. Others mocking said these men are full of wine. 14. But*

Peter, standing up with the eleven, lifted up his voice , and said unto them, Ye men of Judaea, and all ye that dwell at Jerusalem, be it known unto you, and hearken to my words: 15. For these are not drunken, as ye suppose, seeing it is but the third hour of the day. 16. But this is that which was spoken by the prophet Joel; 17. And it shall come to pass in the last days, saith God, I will pour out my Spirit upon all flesh: and your sons and daughters shall prophecy, and your young men shall see visions, and your old men shall dream dreams: 18. And on my servants and on my handmaidens I will pour out in those days of my Spirit: and they shall prophesy:"

In heaven there is a temple. God deemed that earthly replicas should be in the earth as a shadow. Jesus, the earthly embodiment of the heavenly temple, began to fulfill through His earthly ministry what the temples being built in the earth prior to Him could not fulfill. The temples before Him could only do temporally what He alone did eternally. He is our High Priest who ever makes intercession for man.

Jesus having begun what would be continued by His disciples, left the means by which these meager men would light up the entire world. The oil that would trim their lamps would be the comforter who also would charge them to be witnesses for Jesus. The Holy Spirit enables God's people to be used in this way for His purpose in various administrations in the Body of Christ.

I Corinthians 12:4,13,14 *" Now there are diversities, but the same Spirit ". 13. For by one Spirit are we all baptized into one body, whether we be Jews and Gentiles, whether we bond or free; and have been all made to drink into one Spirit. 14. For the body is not one member but many."*

Not only does He enable us by the Holy Spirit to perform our duties, but He also unites us, helping us to maintain order. It all began when the Spirit of God poured out upon the gathered disciples, this started a unifying process which formed the Body of Christ. Nimrod's government displayed the negative parallel of being united. As was Nimrod's people, we should be under Christ as our head, with one central goal in mind, to bring glory to the Father.

The people of Babel were speaking the same language on one accord. This relates to what is taking place in our text, Acts 2:8-12. The only difference is that before Nimrod was able to complete his project, God caused confusion to take place. Remember although it appeared to be order, it was really born out of confusion. Anything not authored by the Lord shall be exposed as confusion.

In the text Acts 2 we see the results of what God started and how it leads to order. The semblance of this was displayed in our text to reveal the contrasting events taking place at the Tower of Babel. The disciples were gathered and they spoke a language which was understood by the masses of people gathered. Such an event brings emphasis to the re-establishing of God's order by His Spirit. The people called the Church received the promise Jesus had promised. The Body of Christ, the temple for God's glory was now filled with His presence. So we enjoin their prayer. Our hope is that as what took place in the Bible represented what took place in heaven, so will heaven's power fall again upon us.

If I were to give an example to highlight our present state, I would use the following. Just imagine, if you can, that a crew of workmen were trying to build a massive structure that required a rigorous and unified effort. Yet, the architect after trying to communicate the plans to the site foreman found out that he didn't understand what he was trying to say. As he tries to communicate, his designs further turning to others on the job site he finds himself faced with the same outcome. This slowly becomes an accumulation of confusion, and the only resolve is to leave the work undone.

We have left the work of building the Church undone. Disabled by our lack of communication we are left ineffective in our efforts to build according to God's pattern. All that we need to do the job is available, but the problem is that the laborers are to few. I am not just referring to the number of people present in the Body of Christ, but also the number of people who are in tune, or are in order with the commonality of the Body to fulfill the will of God.

I am mindful of what some may say to my next comment, so before you jump on me please listen to what I am trying to say. Mega-churches or large church complexes are not a true indication of our being on one accord. Not even grand conferences or elaborate camp meetings are a sign of being on one accord.

The question remains, do we speak alike and hear the same things; this is the test of being on one accord and is indicative of true unity. We've been speaking a broken language and up until now no one has understood us clearly. But when we speak and hear the same, we will build not a place but the people who will stampede into the Church in the latter hour. They need their lives rebuilt and their dreams reconstructed. So the signs on our doors should read " People under renovation", for we are in the business of changing lives for the better.

Let's pray: Father, forgive us for not being in order; Help us to get in place, so we can again be recipients of your Holy Spirit. Fill us, dear God, to the brim until we overflow with power to be on one accord. We want to do Your will at this last day. It's in the name of Jesus Christ, our precious Lord, we pray, Amen.

3.   **The Structure -**

Let us examine what is exactly being built . What does it look like? What material is it made of?

Ephesians 2:10 - *"For we are His workmanship, created in Christ Jesus unto good works, which God hath before ordained that we should walk in them."*

In times past, God formulated the idea of the Church and hid this revelation until He deemed it the right season to unveil this beauty called the Church.

God sent His Spirit to us, the Body of Christ, for more than just saving us from the darkness of this world, but it was His intent that we fulfill His purpose, before the foundations of the world were lain.

Ephesians 4:11-16; *" And He gave some, apostles; and some prophets; and some evangelists; and some pastors and teachers; 12. For the perfecting of the saints, for the work of the ministry, for the edifying of the body of Christ.13. Till we all come in the unity of the faith, and of the knowledge of the Son of God, unto a perfect man, unto the measure of the stature of the fulness of Christ: 14. That we henceforth be no more children tossed to and fro, and carried about with every wind of doctrine, by every sleight of men, and cunning craftiness whereby they lie in wait to deceive; 15. But speaking the truth in love, may grow up into him all things, which is the head, even Christ; 16. From whom the whole body fitly joined together and compacted by that which every joint supplieth, according to the effectual working in the measure of every part, maketh increase of the body unto the edifying of itself in love.* "

a.   **The Five-Fold Offices** -

Like all buildings or structures have a foundation that supports the upper portion of the building, so does the Church. The foundation sets the criteria for the upper levels and is key to the rest of the building's design.

Ephesians 2:19-22; Matt;7;25 b/cl. *"Now therefore ye are no more strangers and foreigners, but fellow-citizens with the saints , and of the household of God. 20. And are built upon the foundation of the apostles and prophets, Jesus Christ himself being the chief cornerstone;21. In whom all the building fitly framed together groweth unto a holy temple in the Lord. 22. In whom ye also are for a habitation of God through the Spirit. ".* Matt.7:25 b/cl. *"For it was founded upon a rock."*

In the Ephesians book, the apostles and prophets with Jesus Christ as the cornerstone make up an aspect of the foundation of the Church. The ministries of evangelists, pastors, and teachers are the next offices making up the foundation.

We read in the text, Ephesians 4:11-16, how the means of the Body's growth is contingent upon these ministries. Apostles and prophets are responsible for establishing and maintaining structure in the Church. Secondly, the evangelists are regarded as the soul winners and traveling soul revivers. Thirdly, seeing that the souls that are won need shepherding, the pastors are called to nurture, to lead, and to further instruct the people in church to get and stay saved. Then finally the teachers in the Body are to aid in the educating of the saints on all matters. The five offices are solely built on the cornerstone Jesus Christ.

I believe this foundation was made unstable numerous times throughout the history of the Church. In particular Jesus addresses the Pharisees and Sadducees about how they were misrepresenting their callings. They should have been stewards of the law. Instead traditions had become the focus of their teachings. Common sayings (Clichés) which were based on compromise became the structure for order . Strangely, if you were apart of the in-crowds, you would be more accepted in society rather than if you had a relationship with God. And to further magnify their instability, when God sent prophets with a word to restore this lost order, they killed them. Jesus rebuked these treacherous acts by calling them white washed walls and a den of vipers on numerous occasions. But they refused to hear even Jesus' words of correction.

Jesus in the book of Matthew 7:25-29 teaches the basis for the foundation of mankind, by maintaining that He is the real foundation called the rock. His lesson refutes the false culture which tried to mask itself as God's order and He further stated that it was only like sinking sand.

The five-fold ministries are the means God has chosen to build up His temple of glory. The core of their assignment involves ministering the word of God as witnesses of Jesus Christ (the cornerstone). The reason why Jesus is the cornerstone is because He is the Word that should be the central theme of society. He declares this to defy the devil in the wilderness by saying, "*man shall not live by bread alone, but by every word that proceedeth out of the mouth of God*." The word liberates humanity to live the standards that are really secure for living.

Faith, real faith, comes by hearing. Hearing, real hearing, only by the word of God, and if there is a word, you must have a preacher. He or she must be sent from God, who speaks those words that will be the foundation of all humanity. The word of God corroborates in the minds of men, the path that is right. It uncovers instability which hides behind a false sense of order in our society. Sin is the menace that erodes our ability to uphold any standard of holiness in this world. The word of God shines as a light dispelling its darkness. God is the Rock of all ages, it's in Him we must trust, hiding His word in our hearts as the foundation. As we preach it on the hilltops, the world will hear, believe and know our God of order.

So, now I am impressed to make a clarion call to those who are the foundation. I implore you to take hold of the helm of your calling and don't take lightly how God has called you. Among you are great pillars of faith. Salvation and sanctification are in your mouths by the Spirit of God. Within your loins lies the welfare of the Church. It is your job to ignite the flame burning within the bosom of the household of faith. This is the signal that will guide humanity from its dark demise.

I, as an emissary of our God, must provoke you to be ever active in your responsibility as you take great reverence knowing its utmost importance. Order dear men and women of God is in your mouths, for the word of God that was spoken in the beginning became as it made an orderly procession out of God's mouth to perform His handiwork. Order then is ordained to again be declared by His anointed servants back into our world. The power of life and death are in our tongues. God has put His word in us by the Holy Spirit's revelation and inspiration. Thus, we are being charged with an awesome responsibility to preach, teach, and prophecy until hell's confusion is abated.

2 Timothy 3:16 *" All scripture is given by inspiration of God, and is profitable for doctrine, for reproof, for correction, for instruction in righteousness."*

The word is so powerful it can carry the Church to the next level of the anointing, the power and the holy integrity of our God. For it will equip us for the task of winning souls to Christ. And as we have all the right tools, with Bibles in our hands, and zeal toward God in our hearts, we must also rest upon "petro," the rock . Then the gates of hell shall not prevail against us, the Church. After which we with steadfastness will be able to stand on our real soap boxes with a word from God, that is not predisposed to political correctness or false piety. Our God-given word will come forth with such power and conviction that people will say, *"How is it that these speak with such authority?"(paraphrased)*

b.   **We all must take part in ministry -**

The baton is being passed to the general assembly from the quote-unquote preachers. We all are built upon them and are together the Body of Christ.

Ephesians 4:12 *"for the perfecting of the saints, for edifying of the Body of Christ."*

There is a role to be assumed for every individual in the Church. As God reforms order in the house at the foundation, He also expects order in the whole house. A chain is only as strong as its weakest link. Therefore, our effectiveness in the house and out of the house is contingent upon all of us doing our parts.

Romans 15:1 " *We then who are strong ought to bear the infirmities of the weak, and not to please ourselves.* "

Apostle Paul knew the importance of this, for he wrote this passage which instructs us to bear the infirmities of those who are weak.

Galatians 6:1 *"Brethren if a brother be overtaken in a fault, ye which are spiritual, restore such a one in the spirit of meekness; considering thyself, lest thou also be tempted."*

He continues this idea in saying that we who are spiritual should restore those overtaken in a fault. When we cover each other like the scripture says, we close any gaps that would create a weakness in the Body. Therefore, the devil finds it harder to make us unstable or out of order with each other and God. So we must be constantly mindful to stay in sync with each other spiritually. Then if our brother or sister is sad, slipping, or stagnant, we will feel them, as its said, to the point of immediately seeking to recover them. We also will be able to support them as they get the victory. We'll get more in to this point later on.

There is a way we can avoid being jealous of our brothers and sisters. It involves taking our place in ministry and fulfilling our individual assignments, thus the whole Body is strengthened to do the work of our God. The Church House is being ushered into an era by God where we will all assume our vocations with excellence and expertise. Then we can launch out into the deep of our destiny to do great exploits for Jesus.

Summary: The all wise, all mighty, and an all-encompassing God would not just allow existence to spin out of control like a movie reel turning without beginning or ending, rattling on noisomely and aimlessly. Although the world is under the direction of an out of control tyrant for a director and the script reads the theme of confusion and mayhem, God has edited the ending so mankind by His grace can make a comeback. God has written a part for His star in the script of time. Our role is to restore order on the scene of humanity. The Church is the only means of restoration of God's order. If we are going to be effective in performing His order, it will have to begin with us first.

Chapter 2.- Where Do We fit In?

If we are called by God for more than just to be saved, what else is there for us? After we've accepted Jesus as Savior and Lord, what are our responsibilities other than coming to church, reading our Bible, and trying to stay saved after we've spent all day fighting the devil and temptations?

In the previous chapter where we discussed the pattern of the temple. We talked about how Moses went into the mountain of God and got a vision from Him, as to the specific details of the temple. Even the workmen were hand-picked by God. Every measurement, the materials and the means were given to Moses for the plan of the temple's construction.

The importance of a vision is as such that it is the key to the Kingdom of heaven and the cities of the world. The Bible emphasizes the vision of the Lord so much that it says without the vision the people will perish. Idle hands are the devil's work shops. An empty mind is free for anything to occupy it. The Lord says, *"Let this mind be in you which was also in Christ Jesus."*

I am saying that we must, at all costs, get a vision from God about where we fit in His Body. Moses talked to God and God talked to him, thus giving him the vision for the temple. When I say talk, I mean we must pray, pray, and pray, waiting for God to speak revelation to our hearts. Our ears must be attentive to write every word God says. For we need to follow God's directions to the "T."

I personally know it works, because when I prayed that prayer, God began to show me who I was and what I shall be. I found out I was called to preach and later He further revealed other details in the days ahead. Such was his revelation to me that I am more knowledgeable about the whom, the what and the why's of my life. No, I don't know it all, but I have perceived enough to be encouraged to go on to see what the end will be.

God has a vision for every area of our lives. Our marriage, our ministry, our business or employment. Let's seek Him until we find and knock until He opens up the answer to our question, "Where do we fit in?" It is important to the destiny of the Body of Christ that the least of us is sure to get into the position God has called us to be in.

Lets pray: Dear God, it is in the Name of Jesus, right now, that I pray for my brothers and sisters. Give them such a thirst and hunger to know where they fit in your Body that they will be driven to go to the heights of heaven. For it is there, oh God, you have the plan for them. I thank You, Jesus, in advance. Amen.

We each depend on what the other has to supply, so the whole Body may increase or, if you will, go higher. It is imperative for the individual person to assume his or her responsibility. That's why it's key for every person to get an understanding of the will of God for themselves so they can properly relate to the Body with their specific calling.

No wonder the devil is busy dividing us. By dividing us he can effectively conquer us. Satan knows that if he can keep even two or three from getting together, he can hinder our effectiveness and, thereby, prevent the will of God for our lives from being accomplished. So this is built on the premise that if he can keep us from getting in our perspective places on one accord he can assimilate us individually easier.

A. **Be Yourself -**

In our endeavor to vocationally be what God has called us to be, we must first understand who we are. It will be hard to unmask what has been covered so long. Because, words have become a tapestry which have shrouded the truth. Our ears have been filled from day one with constant lies, tormenting us until the day we die. We have been so hypnotized by their mesmerizing effects that we have rejected the truth rather than the lie.

The first thread of this cloak over our eyes was woven at the hands of the master craftsman of deception himself. Satan tailored a plan in the Garden of Eden in stitching these lies within the minds of Adam and Eve. This resulted in their off spring being left astray, and further blind folded by the devil's obscurities. So the whole world now is grappling for something to cover their sin. It's comforts have caused them to relax in what won't due. You see, there is no hiding place in darkness from the light of God's truth.

The deception has become so penetrating that our society has tried to perpetuate this illusion. For example, the entertainment industry has spared no expense in creating a world of fantasy to further intoxicate the minds of those that would buy into its euphoric effect. These types of things have preoccupied us with a false world which eventually will cave in around us.

My brother and sister, it is the truth that will make us free. Our first steps trekking toward the truth can only reveal our objective, as it involves Jesus who said, *"I am the way, the truth and the light."* Apostle John also says that He is the Light of men. Light exposes what is obscured by darkness. If any man or woman will know who they are, they must be exposed to the light of Jesus Christ. The psalmist exclaims in Psalm 119:104-105 say, *"Through Thy precepts I get <u>understanding</u>: Therefore, I hate <u>every false way</u>. Thy word is a lamp unto my feet and a <u>light unto my path</u>."*

The truth makes us free, which is the word from God. That word is light or understanding to anyone's path or purpose in life. We first must have Jesus to get on the path of truth which defines who we are and what we are meant to be in Him.

From the beginning, we are made in the image and likeness of God. We are in the world, but are not supposed to be part of the world. The image of God is the reflection we should possess. But we will face a lot of opposition as we attempt to unravel the many facades that have entangled us. Its because the coil's of deception have wrapped around us, causing a further need for personal deliverance.

We may have become Christians, but I've found out that we still need to be in a position of repentance. This allows us to be up front with the truth about ourselves and thus we can align ourselves with the unchanging truth of God. You may be to holy to admit it, but we must forever pray that prayer depicted in Romans 10:9; *"Confess with your mouth the Lord Jesus, and believe in your heart that God raised Him from the dead. (paraphrased)"* Thereby, we can humble ourselves to confess we need redemption. God will expose the lie to reveal in our hearts through His Spirit what's right for us.

If we don't utilize this means of refocusing on who we are, we will continue to be imprisoned in the lie we've lived, becoming submerged in this fake personality and even comfortable with its confusion. If we don't get free, it will further dictate our every move. Church if we get free, it will take God Himself to break through our many masks and shatter our false images of ourselves. Only He can penetrate the callousness of our deceptions which would hide who we are meant to be in God.

Exodus 34:33-35 *"And until Moses had done speaking with them, he put a veil on his face, 34. But when Moses went in before the Lord to speak with Him, he took the veil off, until he came out. And he came out, and he spake unto the children of Israel that which he was commanded. 35. And the children of Israel saw the face of Moses, that the skin of Moses shone: and Moses put the veil upon his face again, until he went to speak with Him."*

Moses is an example of how important it is to be you. He went in the presence of God and unveiled his face so he could be real before the Most High. By being humble and confessing who we are and what we have done, we open ourselves to receive light. This light speaks to understanding or getting a revelation of who we really are. The search light is turned on the depth of our souls. Sin is made known for the purpose of confession. It is also there in God's presence He will speak, not only correction, but also direction as to who we are and how we can enter the process of becoming what and who He has ordained us to be.

This principle is also defined by the scripture reference that says, *"come as you are."* In other words disrobe yourself from the phoney, superficial, and artificial. Adam and Eve were the first to be naked before God. After the serpent instigated sin, they sought to cover who they really were.

*It was God who made us and not we ourselves. Certainly God being omniscient and omnipresent is not ignorant of our covered places. He could see through them like superman can see through a steel shield. Before we were, He was, and now that we are, He still is, and will continue to be. He knew us when we were in our mother's womb. We cannot fool Him. So who do we think we are fooling but ourselves.

1. **Don't Compete, Compare or Covet** -

Genesis 4:3-5,8 *" And in the process of time it came to pass, that Cain brought of the fruit of the ground a offering unto the Lord. 4. And Abel he also brought of the firstlings of his flock and of the fat thereof. And the Lord had respect unto Abel and his offering:5. But unto Cain and to his offering He had not respect. And Cain was very wroth, and his continence fell., "8. And Cain talked with Abel his brother: and it came to pass, when they were in the field , that Cain rose up against Abel his brother, and slew him."*

From the beginning of man's existence, there was an obstacle preventing him from being who God ordained. So much was this obstacle that the infection of sin caused Cain to compete with Abel. This led to Abel's murder at the hands of his angry brother. Cain was so insecure with what he offered God. The rage of jealousy within him was unleashed sealing his fate. But, God still speaks a word meant to correct him; he chose not to adhere to what was his last chance to change. His inadequate feelings with himself eventually drove him to destroy what he felt to be a threat. Cain plotted and carried out the assassination of his blood brother. What he didn't know was that he was original and special in the sight of the Lord. His feeling were hurt, but it had nothing to do with what he did, who he was and what he brought. But it had everything to do with how it was brought. Abel brought the choicest of his flock, *"the firstlings,"* as the Bible says. But Cain just *"bought an offering"* denoting insignificance. God was and is no respecter of persons. But, Cain was so consumed with jealousy that he allowed bitterness in his heart which caused him to be so misguided he began to fight against his own family.

One of our problems, today, is that we are still fighting the wrong enemy. We are killing each other, rather than the real culprit of our confusion. Somebody may be saying, I haven't killed anybody. But, not only can a look kill, but words also can kill. We might not be drawing knives or guns, but we are quick to cut and shoot with slanderous statements about our siblings in Christ Jesus. Once we have hurt the ones we love, the spirit of competition will lead us to being cursed. Then what we were meant to do, we can no longer do, and ultimately, we become an outcast. Moreover, we can't be found in our place in the Body of Christ.

Before Cain competed He **compared** himself to his brother. *This is another attitude believers take which will under mind our identity. When we compare ourselves to others, we make what we have insignificant. We become absorbed and distracted with what other people have to the point of constantly evaluating who has more or less. Like children we cry " That's not fair , they have more than me" or otherwise we teasingly dance in circles saying "Nah, nah, nah, nah, nah- I have some and you don't have none". This can lead to depression or oppression. We cannot be obsessed to possess because we don't have what others have. Or we can't continue to oppress others because they don't have what we assume that we posses. First, we must know, God gives what He wants and how much He wants to whom He pleases. The emphasis must not be on what, how much, or to whom, but on from Whom

James 1:17 *"Every good and perfect gift comes from above and comes down from the Father of lights, with whom there is no variableness or shadow of turning."*

God gives all good and perfect gifts. There aren't any little "I's" and little "you's," all are equally important to Him. For He is most concerned about what you did with what He gave you. Bear fruit in your own season. So what if others can sing, preach, or pray? Do what God gave you to do until it increases. Just get planted beside the still and resourceful waters, God will do the rest. It doesn't matter if you plant one seed or one hundred; all will grow under the proper care. Don't think less of what God has bestowed upon you so graciously. God only gives His best and never less.

*The devil has bred a " keep up with the Joneses" spirit in the Church.

I Corinthians' 3:3 *"For ye are yet carnal; where as there is among you envying, and strife, and divisions, are ye not carnal and walk as men."*

This church at Corinth had the same spirit that typifies one that makes comparisons. We can read the theme of comparing woven throughout Paul's writings to them. First they compared their leaders against each other and then they compared each other's gift. The problem with this attitude is that their focus was on themselves instead of God. Like the Corinthian church, when we lose sight of Christ, sin raises its head in our ranks. Things we normally wouldn't allow to slip through the cracks of our unattended spiritual well being will get in. We, then, discard what is innately most important and begin to observe the external and superficial. All because we want others to see what we have and to see what they don't have. This is the spirit of comparing.

If we want something, we need to speak out of the abundance of our hearts. Then from within, out of the treasure of what God has invested in us, the fruit that will remain can come forth. These are the things that are eternal. The trick of the devil is that he knows the works of the flesh and how it will perish, so he perpetuates the things of the flesh seeking to distract us from the spiritual. The Corinthian's gifts became the emphasis of what they thought was spiritual, but the truth was that they were only external manifestations of the fruit within. They really needed the fruit of the Spirit. We must endeavor to water the inner seed to see the outer fruit.

Man judges the outward appearance and God knows the heart. Where is your heart? David said, *"I hid the word in my heart that I might not sin against God."* Paul said, *"In whatsoever state I am in I've learned to be content."* That means whatever I have, thank you Lord; Who you called me to be, thank you Lord. I have no need to compare; thank you Lord. What's the deal anyway, because in being one with the Body we will benefit from every body's gift in the Church. What's mine is yours, and what's yours is mine. We are so connected that we don't have to compare. Even if I don't have, James writes in Chapter 4:1-3; "***That we have not because we ask not.***"

This attitude eventually moves beyond competing and comparing and it resolves within the heart to take you to the next level of deception. This refusal to seek the source causes us to compare, and further leads to coveting. In James the text expresses some of the reasons for our controversies. We are coveting and wanting what belongs to someone else. These types of people try to keep up but can't. Their obsession drives them further to possess, by any means necessary. It seems that in some way they feel they have a right to get what they have refused to simply ask God for themselves. Don't they know God owns cattle on a thousand hills, the earth is His and the fulness thereof and those that dwell therein.

The seed that breeds coveting is so deep. It's like poison ivy, it's hard to kill. When it springs forth, it does so with a vengeance poisoning everything in its path. In (Exodus 20:17) God boldly commands that we are to covet nothing that belongs to our neighbors. We don't need others' ministry, marriage, songs, gifts, houses, cars, or blessings. God has something especially for us. Don't compete, compare, or covet. Everybody can't be the pastor, preacher, deacon, choir member or missionary. Be yourself, who God is calling you to be. You have a calling in Christ. Please don't pretend to be anything or one else. Don't imitate others, and remember you don't have to entertain to impress the masses. Be yourself.

Tell yourself, others and the devil, "I am whom God says I am!"

Psalm 119:36 *" Incline my heart unto thy testimonies, and not to covetousness."*

2.　　**Jacob Struggled -**

Jacob struggled with who he was. It wasn't easy for him to make the transformation from who he was, to the man God ordained him to be. His story finally heightens to its climax and he is left alone to ultimately face his past and finally be challenged with his future. Will he be or won't he be whom God says? The hosts of angelic witnesses stare from over the edge of heaven's window pane, looking with anticipation as to the decision he will make.

There, Jacob is underneath the starlit sky. The meadow, if you will, as his stage of final reckoning waiting before him. His opponent is in the ring of his destiny with him on the other side. The challenge is for him to change into who he really is. But he must be humbled enough to allow God's will to be exalted in his life. They engaged each other fiercely. Jacob refused to surrender to this worthy challenger. But at the stroke of one move Jacob's walk was changed forever and he would now be crippled and reduced to having to use a walking cane. He was in excruciating pain, but was able to mumble "Who are you", but His opposition's only reply would be the revelation of who Jacob was to be from that day forward. No more Jacob the supplanter or trickster, but now he shall be Israel, the one who struggled with God and prevailed. We like Jacob must struggle against all opposition even ourselves. We are our own worst enemy when it comes to changing.

Yesterday's troubles are often our greatest obstacle. It will take inner fortitude to face our future in spite of our past failures. But, if you hang in there until the breaking of day, God will speak change over your life until you come to yourself.

Jacob is our motif of how a deformed person can be transformed. He made the transition from Jacob to Israel. He moved from potential to power, from trick to triumph, and from a few to a multitude.

B.   **Be Yourself Preacher** -

The only way I can do any justice to this next portion of this book is to tell how God initially spoke to me about being who I am. He used my Bishop and Pastor without him knowing it. At least I don't think he knew it. One day after morning service, I went to Bishop Alfred A. Owens' office and he ask me who prayed during the service. I told him that it was me who prayed. Then, he with a stern, fatherly voice, told me that I sounded like another preacher whose name I won't mention. His next words would penetrate my spirit and find lodging in my heart forever. He said to me, "Be yourself."

Preachers in aspiring to be the best they can be, sometimes struggle with who they are in ministry. There is a propensity, for lack of a better word, to become a copycat preacher. Somewhere between our calling and our final confirmation we become a duplicate of people in our environment. How it happens, I can't figure out, but sure enough we adopt other preacher's mannerisms and gestures.

There isn't a problem with adopting attributes of other people we look up to in the Body of Christ. The problem comes up when we totally lose who we are and how God has called us to be individuals with gifts all of our own. Our personality becomes absorbed and then we won't be able to distinguish between who we are and who others are. Thus, we can never fully blossom into who we really are if we remain this way. Its only because we are living in the shadows of those who tower over us rather than in the light of our gifts.

Therefore, our unique beauty and calling can't be seen, so it can benefit the recipients of our ministry. We dear Brother Preacher and Sister Preacher must be who we were meant to be in Christ.

This may burst your bubble, but all of us can't be T.D. Jakes. Who would do what God has called you to do. As a matter of fact I think Bishop Jakes isn't ready to give up his calling just yet. I was at a birthday celebration for my pastor, Alfred A. Owens, Jr., where T.D. Jakes was the principle speaker. He noted in the introduction of his message that many people were seeking his mantle. But he remarked further that he wasn't through with it yet. While masses of preachers are at the feet of great men or women of God waiting for their mantle, they are missing out on the mantle that belongs to them. Sure God calls some to be armor bearers, and thereby, they may get that mantle. But even Elisha had to tailor Elijah's mantle to his own calling. Just think what he would have missed out on if he chose to do only the equal to Elijah instead of double. Preach to yourself, " I am gonna get what God has for me!"

Proverbs 18:16 *"Wait on the Lord."*

Not only must we be careful to not assume other's personalities, but we also must be careful to not assume to much of ourselves. Anything we do in service to God must be done with sincerity and genuineness. Whether we are praying, preaching, teaching, prophesying, or healing, we must do it with a heartfelt, heart meant and Spirit-led initiative. In other words, preachers you can't force a move of God. I think in our effort to be great and grand sometimes we overstep the boundaries between who we really are and who we are trying to be.

Remember, God isn't at our beck and call, but we are at His. Be mindful that we as ministers of God are so key to the next major move of God that we have got to be in tune to the Lord. Because it is imperative that we function like we are suppose to for the sake of the rest of the Body.

C.   **Be Yourself, Church -**

Once the pew members along with the preachers get in place to be who God has called and ordained them to be, then we as a whole Church must adjust so we will be in order. Then we can be the kind of Church God has predestined us to be.

Matthew 5:13,14 *" Ye are the salt of the earth". "Ye are the light of the world."*

The Church has been lulled into a deep sleep. We are the sleeping beauty of God, waiting for our Prince. He is sounding a clarion call to His people so we will up wake from our lethargic state.

Revelation 3:22. *"He that hath an ear, let him hear what the Spirit saith unto the churches."*

Political correctness has paralyzed us. Therefore, we have lost our identity and have become colored with the polluted ideals of the society we live in. We aren't suppose to be of the world, but we are.

Ephesians 5:14 *" Wherefore He saith, Awake thou that sleepest, and arise from the dead, and Christ shall give thee light."*

The above text alludes to how our eyes were once closed. But now it is high time for us to wake up and be who God said we should be. Whatever has intoxicated us, causing us to stumble at the purpose

God has for the Church must be exchanged with what can sober us to the present cause of God in this last day.

Prayer: Kiss us, sweet Prince of Peace, that the Church you call your bride might rise from her drunken stupor and stand fast and unmoveable, always abounding in your work. Cover our sins, let the breath of Your Spirit revive us to be empowered to do greater works and grand exploits.

In the previous chapter, we talked about order being established and how it happened. As we go on, I pray that God has His way as He quickens us with His Spirit. By His Holy Spirit He can reveal to us the deep things leading us into all of His truth. Thus we can expose the lies and know the truth.

1.   **We are who God Says We Are** -

No word God has spoken will return void unto Him. He's not a man that He should lie, nor the son of man that He should repent. Heaven and earth shall pass away, but our God's word shall last forever. We must internalize this truth about God when thinking about what He has specifically said to us individually and corporately. God has said words over His Church that profoundly describe our appearance and occupation in this world.

In the text Matt 5:13,14 we specifically read what Jesus has declared about us. These words will be our guide in being who we are suppose to be. They will also aid us in understanding what it is we should be doing.

Light is indicative of the character that Jesus displayed during His earthly ministry. He passes this same fiery torch of service to us for the express reason of being a living testament to who He is before a world that lives in darkness. Salt also depicts how we must season man-kind by way of the Preserver, Jesus. Being the light, we have become beacons of hope in the midst of this world. People in it can't see for themselves because of sin.

Light also speaks to the wisdom we have been given through God's word which is the lamp unto our pathway. Salt speaks to eternity which will defy all decay eroding man's souls into the pit of hell. You are the salt of the earth and the light of the world. Be who God said you are.

1.   Priest and Levite Do Your Jobs -

Luke 10:30-34 *" And Jesus answering said, A certain man went down from Jerusalem to Jericho, and fell among thieves, which stripped him of his raiment, and wounded him, and departed, leaving him half dead. 31. And by chance there came down a certain priest that way; and when he saw him, he passed by the other side. 32. And likewise a Levite, when he was at the place, came and looked on him, he passed by the other side. 33. But a certain Samaritan, as he journeyed , came and looked; and when he saw him, he had compassion on him. 34. And he went to him, and bound up his wounds, pouring in oil and wine, and set him on his own beast, and brought him to an inn, and took care of him."*

The Church has a responsibility for which God is holding us liable. In the above text, God revealed to me the parallel between the Priest and Levite, and the Church. As well as the Samaritan and our own modern-day government. The wounded person represents the lost souls of this world and also struggling saints who are left by the waste side of life to perish.

I don't know how some of you may feel about it, but I don't think its all right to leave hurting and hopeless people for dead. We've got to change this attitude in the Church. God has left us to be responsible for these people, not the Samaritans or the government.

The Samaritans were a group of people who were separated from the commonwealth of Israel. That's why the Samaritan woman was shocked when Jesus asked her for water since Jews did not associate with Samaritans. (John 4:9) Yet we read how this alienated Samaritan found it in his heart to do what the Church folk should have been doing. God is calling us to step up to the plate and do what is ours to do. The government is about to stop its programs and welfare support to the wounded of this society. They are shutting them down even as we speak. Who, then, will be their light and salt (means of survival)? Let the redeemed of the Lord say so or, if you will, say something, lest the words which are balm never be administered to heal the slain and the dying. God so loved the world that He gave His only begotten Son (the word). What will we do?

We who are considered the parallels of the Priest and Levite must rise with the word of God (Christ) to minister reconciliation between God and man. No, everybody can't and aren't called to preach. But there is a sermon in you that can witness to the world. There is a touch that only you have that will heal the leper's of their disease.

Looking at our next talk, we must know that collectively we are called to perform wonders and miracles. But we are being hindered from moving in the full flow of the anointing God wants to pour on and through the corporate Church. Rigor mortis or rather rituals have stifled our forward movement. We are frozen in time, because we have turned back from the plow. Now we are like a pillar of salt that has lost its savor. Our only worth is to be trampled under the feet of swine. Deliver us, Lord Jesus!

2.   De-Church the Church -

Ezekiel 33:8-9   I am also concerned that when and if we finally wise up and begin to do our job, people won't really listen to our words of deliverance, healing, salvation, and revival? Faith does come by hearing.

In Eziekiel 33:31,32 it describes a common present-day occurrence. It describes how people get in the habit of just coming to where the word is being preached. They hear the audible sounds of our voices and they are entertained unto enchantment. The next text envelopes this thought.

Ezekiel 33:31-32   *"31. But they do not do them, for with their mouth they show love, but their hearts pursue their own gain, 32. for they hear your words, but they do not do them."*

I wonder, are people just going through the motions rather than being in motion in the Church? I sense that something has happened to stop up our ears and to weigh down our shoes so we can't preach and walk in the gospel of peace. Thus we are challenged to discuss how we must de-church our Church, so we can come alive to do what we have heard.

Preachers our goal has to be that people respond to what they purport to be hearing, rather than to just talk with nobody really listening.

Acts 2:44-47 - 44 *"And all that believed were together, and had all things in common; 45. And sold their possessions and goods, and* *parted them to all men, as every man had need. 46. And they, continuing daily with one accord in the temple, and breaking bread from house to house, did eat their meat with gladness and singleness of heart(NKJV, <u>simplicity of heart</u>), 47. Praising God, and having favour with all the people. And the Lord added to the church daily such as should be saved."*

As we seek to fulfill all the purposes of God unto which we are called as a Body of Believers, we should be compelled to better understand the means and methods by which we can. This leads us to look at the above text in our search for an answer.

Prayer: "God show us how we can be all you have called us to be as we seek direction and connection. Order our steps in your will for us, the Church."

A lot of word is being taught, preached and prophesied in this era of the Church. I don't know if there are others who feel like I do, but I've become restless with words and works of mere men. I am getting to a place where it's becoming apparent to me that only God can speak what we need to hear. Speak Lord. Speak to our hearts what we need to hear.

Looking at the book of Acts, we read about a move of God taking place that we have to envy today. We don't see it happening as often as it occurred then. The full measure of God's power isn't apparently being experienced in the Church today. Only a portion of the Church is moving in this realm of the anointing. I can't say how many because God hasn't shown me that, but we have yet to reach our peak throughout the whole Church.

Whatever happened to the flow of power that was occurring initially in the Church movement. The Bible records this powerful experience of the Church, yet somewhere and somehow we lost a page in history that would link us to the early disciples.

Jesus begins speaking, promising His disciples that they will receive power after the Holy Ghost comes upon them and, as a result of this encounter, they will be His witnesses in Jerusalem, Judea, Samaria and to the uttermost parts of the earth. This promise was also to the present-day Church. For we also are His disciples and are being submitted to this commission.

Chapter two of Acts allows us to read the beginning of the fulfillment of the Lord's promise. This group of devout Christians were praying on one accord with each other and waiting in anticipation of who was to come. The atmosphere in the people packed room was one of common devotion and mutual desire. After fifty days the promise finally came and filled the room and its occupants with power from on high. The immediate result of having this power is consequently seen in the lives and ministries of these avid followers of the risen Savior. Souls are saved when they hear the preached word out of the mouths of these unlearned disciples. The spirit of harmony and togetherness most characterizes these newly formed believers. They had a common goal and good in mind. They are determined to serve the Lord in simplicity.

Analyzing our present condition as a worldwide Church, I risk being called a critic. We must diagnose the reasons we lack the power described in the Scriptures. If we are honest, we will admit that we've waned from our former works. Some how we've gotten comfortable with being this way. If we are going to get in God's order, we again must encounter a move of the Holy Ghost at this magnitude.

I believe this is one of my main assignments in writing this book. To focus on provoking the Church to seek the power of God that we have not fully experienced in the whole Body at the same time. God has revealed to me some of the reasons for our present dilemma.

Personally I have recognized that the absence of God's presence has made my heart grow fonder of Him. In turn this has caused me to cry out for God to change me and move me forward into another realm of His glory. With everything in me, I am fighting against the form of religiosity. It has been here in this desert place that I have learned to hear God speaking a word of deliverance not only for me, but the entire Church.

Some of us in the Body of Christ have allowed ourselves to be subjected to a form and fashion. This has lead to a decrease or even a total loss of fervor. Summing it up, we have become what I call "churchy." A traditional way of thinking has caused us to become insensitive to God's Spirit. Oh yeah, we shout on the cue when the music is played and we have developed a knack for quickening at the right moment. Don't be fooled it's only being churchy and not Church.

We have all the church vernacular down packed. All our amens are said at the right time. We say "Praise the Lord" without meaning and sincerity. When we speak to our brothers and sisters, it is so mechanical and without a true concern for them. Thus, we have become submerged in an atmosphere of church-iness.

This church-y environment sets a conducive tone for vile godlessness. So it's easier to just go through the motions and seek the form more than the Father. The form is comfortable; It says why move or change. Its fine right here. It doesn't seek better or more, but settles for what used to be. People caught in the web of a form which leads to godlessness are trapped by its lie. When God has moved we are still stuck and left empty, and void of the presence of God. We then miss the next level God wants to elevate us to.

The problem this further will pose is that the anointing we were used to slaying lions and bears with yesterday, won't kill the giants we presently face today.

The new King James version uses the word *simplicity* of heart in place of singleness of heart. I speak of simplicity, because we have become so complicated with our drama in the Church. No, I am not referring to plays or theater shows themselves. But I am talking about some of our fronting attitudes. In other words we have gotten in God's way with our extra baggage. We are an obstruction to the free flow of the Holy Ghost in the Church. We are doing a lot that has nothing to do with what God wants done. Thus the eternal move of God has been reduced to the few moments with men. What ever we do, we must hear God and do what He has said to do.

As we remove ourselves from a form of godliness and return to simplicity as the text describes, we then can resume a position of power in our midst. Simplicity speaks to humility, and humility suggests to us reverence for God alone. That's simple. If I be lifted up I will draw all men unto me. Let God arise and His enemies will scatter. I must decrease so He will increase.

The text in Acts 2 says that as a direct result of this simplistic concept, the disciples were able to continue steadfastly in the apostle's doctrine and fellowship, breaking bread, and being in prayers. Tithes and offerings weren't a problem. No needs went unmet, and they were on one accord in the Church as they praised the Lord together and consequently the Lord added to the Church those that were being saved. This is the way the Church should be flowing today.

Prayer: "God get us out of the clutches of the form of godliness and move us back or rather forward to a place of power. Help us to be simplistic so that we can again experience an abundance in the Church, Amen."

What is our solution to getting out of the forms of life? The Father doesn't require form in the Church, but He does require faith.

Hebrews 11:6 *"But without faith it is impossible to please him; for he that cometh to God must believe that he is, and that he is a rewarder of them that diligently seek him."*

Faith which seeks the Father will break through all traditions and any mold to get to the Father. Faith, I mean real faith, will disregard ones personal feelings and other's private opinions to be in His presence. Faith forges fronts and leaps over facades to be real enough to humble yourself. It says "I'll do whatever it takes."

Moses, for example, who was seeking the Father opened the veil that was between he and God. He did all he could to get to Who he knew would be his strength and hope. The Church must turn in an about face from our present decline and do what we must by God's Spirit and grace to change our attitudes. If the Church will be rid of this subtle corrosive erosion of our power, we must overthrow this enemy by the Power of God. This is a mind set which has become a stronghold preventing us from being the Church whom God has called for such a time as this.

This Church is arrayed in the visible brilliance of God's glory, shining forth as a light unto the world. It lifts God above all else and pursues Him with all sincerity and truth. This Church is a bride, indeed. And the groom would be proud and pleased with her. She is His virtuous woman, for she does all to please her Lord. This Church is so subservient that in honor of Him, she is bent in reverent worship to get to Him. The cost doesn't matter for her. She just wants the atmosphere to change around her. She is even willing to break the alabaster box in her hand. Nothing can restrain this woman from worshiping to get free from the forms that held her before. If we duplicate her acts, we will be de-churched. The real Church can be delivered from its confines, when we get back to basics. Worship God in Spirit and in truth, for God seeks such to worship Him.

Summary: God uniquely can not lie. He defies what we hear, see and know about anything in the world. If our God said it, that settles it, and no one can change what He has ordained before time began. He has declared who and what people and things shall be. We like the fig tree Jesus rebuked until it withered, must produce, doing what he said or we will be left to recede. The fruit that will benefit all existence must come forth out of us, as we are who God says we should be. The plan of God is to save the lost, for His will is that no man should perish.

Chapter 3. - United We Stand

Matthew 12:25-28 *"25. And Jesus knew their thoughts, and said unto them Every kingdom divided against itself is brought to desolation; and every city or house divided against itself shall not stand. 26. And if Satan cast out Satan, he is divided against himself; how shall then his kingdom stand? 27. And if I by Beelzebub cast out devils, by whom do your children cast them out? Therefore they shall be your judges. 28. But if I cast out devils by the Spirit of God, then the kingdom of God is come unto you."*

There can't be order in God's house if we ourselves are in disarray against each other. We will have to take a united stand, lest we be left in our own ruins to never be a monument unto God's glory. We must stand tall in this world as a watchtower beckoning men to Christ.

In our above text chapter, we must deal with what has kept us and will keep us apart. As a result this has hindered us from doing what we can only achieve as a unit under Christ Jesus the head of the

Church. There is good reason for us to come together. It is urgent and detrimental to the future of our existence as the Church of God.

A.   <u>We Need Each Other -</u>

I Corinthians 12:21-27 *"And the eye cannot say unto the hand, I have no need of thee; nor again the head to the feet, I have no need of you. 22. Nay, much more those members of the body, which seem to be more feeble, are necessary. 23. And those members of the body which we think to be less honorable, upon these we bestow more abundant honour; and our uncomely parts have more abundant comeliness. 24. For our comely parts have no need; but God hath tempered the body together having given more abundant honour to that part which lacked: 25. That there should be no schism in the body; but that the members should have the same care one for another. 26. And whether one member suffer, all the members suffer with it; or one member be honoured, all the members rejoice with it. 27. Now ye are the body of Christ, and members in particular."*

Contrary to the cliche that states "one monkey don't stop no show," we need each other to the point we cannot disregard even the least among the parts of the Body. As a matter of fact, the above text illustrates that we should ascribe more importance to those often considered less valuable to the whole.

The Corinthian Church was in a state of confusion because of this attitude they conveyed toward each other. Paul, knowing the importance of our unity, rebuked this spirit among them by writing this portion of scripture. He drew attention to the areas where we are common or alike, and encouraged them to share in each other's sadness and victories. He didn't want them to focus on the issues that would divide them and, thereby, frustrate their efforts to come together.

Church we must understand the necessity of our brothers and sisters in Christ as it relates to you getting where you should be. Look at this example in the book of Acts.

Acts, 6:2-4 *"Then the twelve called the multitude of the disciples unto them, and said, It is not reason that we should leave the word of God, and serve tables. 3. Wherefore, brethren, look ye out among you seven men of honest report, full of the Holy Ghost and wisdom, whom we may appoint over this business. 4. But we will give ourselves continually to prayer, and to the ministry of the word."*

So we see the importance of the deacons and how their responsibilities enabled the apostles to do their assignments efficiently. No matter what their role is, other people in Christ, doing their part in the Body enables all of us to do what God has called us to do. If you don't think so, cut off your hands and see how hard it will be to eat, wash or do the simplest task. We need each other Church of God!

How do we then stay together? What will enable us to maintain our oneness like mortar that holds a brick building together?

John 15:9-17 *"As the Father hath loved me, so have I loved you; Continue ye in my love. 10.If ye keep my commandments; ye shall abide in my love, even as I have kept my Father's commandments, and abide in his love. 11. These things have I spoken unto you, that my joy might remain in you, and that your joy might be full. 12. This is my commandment, That ye love one another, as I have loved you. 13. Greater love hath no man than this, that a man lay down his life for his friends. 14. Ye are my friends, if ye do whatsoever I command you. 15. Henceforth, I call you not servants; for the servant knoweth not what his lord doeth; but I have called you friends; for all things that I have heard of my Father I had made known unto you. 16. Ye have not chosen me, but I have chosen you, and ordained you, that ye should go and bring forth fruit, and that your fruit should remain; that whatsoever ye shall ask of the Father in my name, he may give it you. 17. These things I command you, that ye love one another."*

Love gives adhesiveness to the Body of Christ. And it is the means by which we can maintain our integrity. Love reaches out to grasp and hold another. It seeks to establish a bond with another. It overlooks differences and tries to make an amends. Love unites, because it appreciates and celebrates others.

I Corinthians 13:1-8a. *"Though I speak with tongues of men and angels, but have not love, I have become sounding brass or a clanging cymbal. 2. And though I have the gift of prophecy, and understand all mysteries and all knowledge, and though I have all faith, so that I could remove mountains, but have not love, I have nothing. 3. And though I bestow all my goods to feed the poor, and though I give my body to be burned, but have not love, It profits me nothing. 4. Love suffers long and is kind; love does not envy; love does not parade itself, is not puffed up; 5. does not behave itself rudely, does not seek its own, is not provoked, thinks no evil; 6. does not rejoice in iniquity, but rejoices in truth; 7. bears all things, believes all things, hopes in all things, endures in all things. 8. Love never fails -"*

Love, contrary to our talents or gifts, keeps us together. There are churches filled with God's anointed singers, musicians, deacons, missionaries and preachers of every sort, but these gifts are lost on the list of the things attributed to us being as one. Yes, we are one in the Spirit, but the fruit of the Spirit are responsible more than the gifts of the Spirit. Men and women of God, let's be mindful to endeavor to love each other as Christ commands us to. Because we need each other to do the will of God.

B.   **Sibling Rivalries -**

If love gets us together, what keeps us apart? One of the key hindrances which creates a wedge between us to keep us apart is not an outside invader, as some might think, but the true source of our division is sibling rivalries.

Genesis 4:4-10 *"And Abel, he also brought of the firstlings of his flock and of the fat thereof, and the Lord had respect unto Abel and to his offering; 5. But unto Cain and to his offering he had not respect. And Cain was very wroth, and his countenance fell. 6. And the Lord said unto Cain, Why art thou wroth? And why is thy countenance fallen? 7. If thou doest well, shalt thou not be accepted? And if thou doest not well, sin lieth at the door. And unto thee shall be his desire, and thou shalt rule over him. 8. And Cain talked with Abel his brother; and it came to pass, when they were in the field, that Cain rose up against Abel his brother, and slew him. 9. And the Lord said unto Cain, Where is Abel thy brother? And he said, I know not: Am I my brother's keeper? 10. And he said, What has thou done? The voice of thy brother's blood crieth unto me from the ground."*

Prayer: Father, in the Name of Jesus, I pray that you anoint every word, phrase, and paragraph of this next segment. Let the words find a place in the hearts of every reader. Let no word be unfruitful, but let the fruit in this manuscript bring forth that which remains. I rebuke every interference from the devil and his demons right now and, I pray, the Holy Spirit navigates this message to its destination and until it is applied. Let hearts be left rent in your presence and reconciliation be our proclamation in victory. In Jesus' Name, I pray, Amen.

As I was sitting watching a television program in the comfort of my home, I was in awe at the stellar performances of the actors. The story's main theme was that of two brothers who, from a very early age, were in a struggle against each other. A rivalry brewed between them and they were often at odds throughout the story. As the script climaxed, in one final eruption of bitterness between the brothers. It leads to a tear-jerking scene, where the two brothers ended up embracing each other with tears in their eyes. They realized that burying the hatchet would be their solution to a life-long drama.

God began to speak to my heart concerning how this represented the status of the Church, as it too, lies in a position of sibling rivalries. From the beginning of humanity and the establishment of its societies, we see this common conflict in families.

Cain and Abel are the first bad examples for brothers, they were not able to come to the table and negotiate peace. Cain competed with his brother Abel for the attention of God, yet the problem wasn't that God was bias toward him in particular, but that He was partisan against the purity of his gift. Cain could have had what Abel had if he would have just done what Abel did.

Like Cain, some of us are admiring other's positions with God, but we must curtail our ways and understand some simple principles

God requires. One principle is that God requires each of us to be sanctified in all that we do, giving Him priority. The second principle is that God is a God of timing and seasons. We must wait on our time and our own season to receive our personal blessing.

Psalm 1:1-6 *"Blessed is the man that walked not in the counsel of the ungodly, nor standeth in the way of sinners, not sitteth in the seat of the scornful. 2. But his delight is in the law of the Lord; and in his law doth he meditate day and night. 3. And he shall be like a tree planted by the rivers of water, that bringeth forth his fruit in his season; his leaf also shall not wither; and whatsoever he doeth shall prosper; 4. the ungodly are not so; but are like the chaff which the wind driveth away. 5. Therefore the ungodly shall not stand in the judgment, nor sinners in the congregation of the righteous. 6. For the Lord knoweth the way of the righteous; but the way of the ungodly shall perish."*

God rewards those who diligently seek Him and seek first the kingdom of God and all His righteousness.

Then, He adds James 4:1-3 *"From whence comes wars, and fightings among you? Come they not hence, even of your lusts that war in your members? 2. Ye lust, and have not; ye kill, and desire to have, and cannot obtain; ye fight and war, yet ye have not, because ye ask not. 3. Ye ask, and receive not, because ye ask amiss, that ye may consume it upon your lusts."*

Sometimes and maybe even most of the time, it's as simple as asking with the right attitude.

Matthew 7:7-11 *"Ask, and it shall be given you; Seek, and ye shall find; Knock, and it shall be opened unto you: 8. For every one that asketh receiveth, and he that seeketh findeth; and to him that knocketh it shall be opened. 9. Or what man is there of you, whom if his son ask bread, will he give him a stone? 10. Or if he ask a fish, will he give him a serpent? 11. If ye then, being evil, know how to give good gifts unto your children, how much more shall your Father which is in heaven give good things to them that ask him?"*

God doesn't want to withhold what He has for us. He is not aloof in heaven sneering at us with His nose up in the air as if He uses blessings to manipulate men and women. God freely gives to those that ask. Then there is no fear in what He will give because every good and perfect gift comes from above. Our God has our best interest at heart, even to the point that we don't have to be anxious for anything, but we can simply let our request be made known to Him.

There is no need to fight amongst ourselves because God has something for each of us. For example in the beginning of Genesis 25:21-34, we read about the controversy that had been going on between Esau and Jacob from birth. Esau and Jacob struggled for the attention of their father, Isaac, who favored Esau the most. Finally, tension built up to one paramount showdown, when Jacob tricked Esau to agree to give up his birthright. Esau was so infuriated that he threatened his brother with murder. Therefore, Jacob was hustled out of town by a fearful mother, who had supported her youngest son's treachery against his brother.

After reaping what he had sown years later, Jacob, again, must confront his brother, but he was fearful, for he remembered his brother's last words to him threatening his life. Jacob, forced to seek a solution, sought God whom he knew would be the answer to his impending danger ahead.

As we look at our text now, it must be noted that although Esau had complained about what he thought Jacob stole; he now refuses his brother's humble offer for him to accept gifts of recompense. His reason blows my mind with a revelation from God. Esau said, "*I have enough; keep what you have for yourself*." He had so much he didn't miss what Jacob stole.

My brother and sister, what God has for you is for you. No one else can fill your shoes or wear the mantle God has anointed for you alone. It's personal what God does for us individually.

Go ahead and expose what the sources of your rivalries are with your brother or sister in Christ. Because, how can two walk together except they agree with each other? We need each other, so we must be united at all costs. This means that we must put away our childish differences for the greater cause ahead.

C.   **Net + Work = Network -**

We must recognize our need for each other and expel what causes schisms in the Body of Christ. Coming together, we will be able to accomplish greater exploits for God. Our paramount feat for the future of the Church is to get on one accord.

Luke 5:1-11 (6, 7) *"And it came to pass, that, as the people pressed upon him to hear the word of God, he stood by the Lake of Gennesaret, 2. and saw two ships standing by the lake; but the fishermen were gone out of them, and were washing their nets. 3. And he entered into one of the ships, which was Simon's, and prayed him that he would thrust out a little from the land. And he sat down, and taught the people out of the ship. 4. Now when he had left speaking, he said unto Simon, Launch out into the deep, and let down you nets for a draught. 5. And Simon answering said unto him, Master, we have toiled all the night, and have taken nothing; nevertheless at thy word I will let down the net. 6. And when they had this done, they inclosed a great multitude of fishes; so that they began to sink. 8. When Simon Peter saw it, he fell down at Jesus' knees, saying, Depart from me; for I am a sinful man, O Lord. 9. For he was astonished, and all that were with him, at the draught of fishes which they had taken; 10. And so was also James, and John, the sons of Zebedee, which were partners with Simon. And Jesus said unto Simon, Fear not; from henceforth thou shalt catch men. 11. and when they had brought their ships to land, they forsook all, and followed him."*

Here in the above text Jesus is speaking a word to Peter that is relative to the Church finding souls. Like Peter we need to have sensitive ears that are attentive to the voice of our Master in these last days. If the Church will reap this latter-day harvest, we must be in a place with God in order to listen. He that wins souls is wise, not with earthly wisdom, but with wisdom that comes from God alone.

The other thing that obstructs the Church from gathering the harvest or doing any of the duties God has assigned to us is found in the 6th and 7th verse. There we read how Peter does what Jesus commanded; he cast his net in anticipation of what would follow. He caught a large amount of fish, which Jesus later likened unto catching men by saying to the new disciples, He would make them fishers of men. The part of this text I need to highlight is where Peter's net broke and for fear of losing the catch, he called over to his fellow fishermen to help him retrieve those that would be lost. The combination proved to be successful. The revelation God has shown here is relative to the unification of the Church in our working relationship.

God wants the net and the work to come together. The people of God must network our talents, resources, skills, gifts, callings and anointing to catch the harvest of souls in these last days.

For example, if God has given it to a pastor to rehabilitate drug abusers and, yet, he lacks the skill to minister healing to the HIV infected of his community, it would behoove him to call to a man or woman of God who is gifted and called in this area, least those souls be lost. We must network to make the Church work in order.

Others marvel that God has blessed some to do so well financially, but I am quickly saddened when I see other ministries lacking. The strong must bear the infirmities of the weak, so we all can be strengthened as a body. We are our brother's keepers. Once we network, every joint will be able to supply an increase to the whole Body. Then, we will be functioning in the order God has ordained for us from the beginning.

Ecclesiastes 4: 12 *"And if one prevail against him, two shall withstand him; and a threefold cord is not quickly broken."*

There is another example given in the book of Nehemiah starting in, chapter 2:5-8. This story starts with one man that had a burden to rebuild what was ordained by God from the beginning. The plans and design had already been given to God's people, they only needed to do what had already been done.

Note that Nehemiah started by first getting permission from the king. Before we rebuild the Church we will have to ask our King for permission and then we must ask for the materials we need. Secondly this man of vision had the gumption to spearhead this seemingly impossible campaign to rebuild. What I mean by this is that if we wait on the vote to come in nothing will ever get done. We need the pioneers of the Church to stand up. What are you waiting for? Following the history of almost all revivals, we see that they started with one person or a small group. It took only Jesus and twelve men to turn an entire world upside down. It took one man named Seymour and a small group in a house church to set a nation ablaze with the power of the Holy Ghost on Izusa street. It must start somewhere and it must start. It might as well be with us. If two or three will gather in Jesus' name, there He will be in the midst. In the previous text Peter started and others followed as he followed Jesus.

Next in Nehemiah 2:11-18, Nehemiah assessed the damages when he went at night to look at the ruins. He had to account for the proper repairs. The very next day he got on his soap box and reported the condition of the wall to the people with hopes to provoke them to want to help him rebuild.

Now this is where we begin to see the networking in action. We as a people must hear the words of our Nehemiahs, preaching rebuild to us. It must come as a sound of rushing wind to bring us on one accord to do the work. Only what is order can change what is in disorder. Such is a word from God.

In chapter 2: 19-20, Nehemiah refuses to allow those who had no inheritance in Israel to partake in rebuilding. In other words, only those in agreement with the common wealth of the Church can work. We can't use worldly tactics, or worldly agendas, or even worldly people. Now I know the wealth of the rich is laid up for the righteous, but it does not mean the same thing. In this case, the Spirit of the movement must flow without diversions. How can two walk together except they be agreed? Nehemiah used other nation's materials but he didn't ask anybody but God's people to rebuild. This is the only way the net will work. Although Nehemiah began a good work, the work didn't mean a thing without the people who made up the net. The scripture says that *"the people had a mind to work."*

There is one other example I would like to use to hit this point home. In the book of Judges chapters 6-8. The networking system is in the innate anointed talents and gifts we all have individually. We won't ever unite because of our external color or denominational signs outside of our Church doors. Christ in us is the hope of glory.

More specifically we will be dealing with chapter 6:16, *"And the LORD said unto him, Surely I will be with thee, and thou shalt smite the Midianites as <u>one man</u>,."* This is where Gideon the man of valor is our subject matter. Again we read how God wants to use the people as one unit. Briefly the story dealt with God breaking down what was initially a large group responding to Gideon's request to go to war. Trouble had brought them together to do one thing, survive. But everybody couldn't fight, so the mountain becomes a mold hill with only three hundred men left from the multitude. The rationale of God was that He wanted people to know He fought the battle against the enemy. It only takes a few who are on one accord. I wish we would get this concept like the people of the world have. Because, once we unite under the banner of Christ; we will be able to fully harness all of the parts in the body to the glory of God by the grace of the Holy Spirit. **Net + Work = Network**

Summary: No man or woman is an island. God even in His being is not alone, but three as one entity are operating in the God-head. We are a reflection of our God and thus must put away our -isms and schisms. We are blood relatives who are bought with the same price. If what our Lord has required of us will be done, we must get connected to each other. This is how we will be able to put each other's gifts, callings and anointing to their best use to all.

Chapter 4.- We Must Resume Our Position

God is doing something in the midst of the Church community to cause us to return to our former works. It was in a town called Antioch where we most resembled what God had ordained from the beginning. Truly we have been deformed by our toxic environment since then, and several times over. God is taking us through sort of a spiritual cosmetic surgery to give us a face lift. He wants to restore the image that was lost, so we will be in the image of Christ, our Lord. Transformation for the purpose of reformation and, therefore, we can reach our long-awaited destination. This is the meaning of order in the Church.

We must resume our position. The caravan awaits us; others have already boarded, but we all must take our seats, for this must be a corporate effort.

A.   **The Gathering -**

Ephesians 1:10   *"That in the dispensation of the fulness of times he might gather together in one all things in Christ, both which are in heaven, and which are on earth; Even in him.*

God has predestined, within the counsel of His own will, that all should be gathered together in Christ. He is tempering together those that normally wouldn't be together; Baptist walking with Pentecostal, and Pentecostal with A.M.E. and A.M.E. with Apostolic, and so on. God not only is cross-uniting denominations, but He is also doing this culturally, socially and economically; barriers are being broken down to ignite the era of the gathering. Everything that would divide us is being removed so we can come together. Our nucleus of unity is Christ. He is the magnet to bring opposites into one arena for a common purpose. We have been flying under the banner of our individual movements to long. It is time for us to assess our out-of-order posture and swiftly reform under whom we are truly indivisible.

Genesis 45:1-15 *"Then Joseph could not refrain himself before all those who stood by him; and he cried, Cause every man to go out from me. And there stood no man with him, while Joseph made himself known to his brethren. 2. And he wept aloud: and the Egyptians and the house of Pharaoh heard. 3. And Joseph said unto his brethren, I am Joseph; doth my father yet live? And his brethren could not answer him; for they were troubled at his presence. 4. And Joseph said, I am Joseph, your brother, whom ye sold into Egypt. 5. Now therefore be not grieved, nor angry with yourselves, that ye sold me hither; for God did send me before you to preserve life. 6. For these two years hath the famine been in the land: and yet there are five years, in which there shall neither be earing nor harvest. 7. And God sent me before you to preserve you a posterity in the earth, and to save your lives by a great deliverance. 8. So now it was not you that sent me hither, but God:*

and he hath made me a father to Pharaoh, and lord of all his house, and a ruler throughout all the land of Egypt. 9. Haste ye, and go up to my father, and say unto him, Thus saith thy son Joseph, God hath made me lord of all Egypt: come down unto me, tarry not: 10. And thou shalt dwell in the land of Goshen, and thou shalt be near unto me, thou, and thy children, and thy children's children, and thy flocks, and thy herds, and all that thou hast: 11. And there will I nourish thee; for yet there are five years of famine; lest thou, and they household, and all that thou hast, come to poverty. 12. And, behold, your eyes see, and the eyes of my brother Benjamin, that it is my mouth that speaketh unto you. 13. And ye shall tell my father of all my glory in Egypt, and of all that ye have seen; and ye shall haste and bring down my father hither. 14. And he fell upon his brother Benjamin's neck, and wept; and Benjamin wept upon his neck. 15. Moreover he kissed his brethren, and wept upon them: and after that his brethren talked with him."

It is written how Joseph suffered a lot of harm from his brothers. He had many reasons to hold a grudge against them. They assaulted his integrity, maligned his dreams, put him in a pit and left him for dead and, finally, he was sold to slave traders and carried to Potifer's house. There he further was stripped of his dignity and abased by lies and sent to jail for a crime he didn't commit. In prison, underneath Pharaoh's palace, he mulled over this rejection. What I am trying to show you is that Joseph could have easily developed a "how do you like me now" spirit.

Some of us have been hurt by our relatives in Christ. Harsh words have been weapons to put us in pits and prisons. The Church has been at each other's throats for many reasons, but none are good enough to continue to hold a grudge. God used Joseph's trials to build his testimony and its by the blood of the Lamb and the power of our testimony that we can overcome anything. Joseph couldn't be who he was unless his brothers did what they did against him. God was behind the scenes orchestrating what was meant for evil in Joseph's life to turn it into good for His glory.

We, too, must recognize the hand of our Lord in our times of trouble. I believe God was behind the Church's season in the valley. It was there He was preparing us for the promise. The devil doesn't get the credit, because God will let no one glory in His presence. God has used a famine, the lack of a word from Him. Without it we have no sustenance. For this reason, we have found ourselves together in one place. Hunger for God has driven us beyond the walls of our traditions and denominations. The white banner of holiness flying in the wind of the Holy Spirit has been raised. This has become our common pledge, and for it we have stood in lines to enter crowded conference halls. The most ridiculed among us is being raised to bless the rest. God is lifting the down trodden to be the means of inciting the movement of reconciliation. The reason isn't to exalt one group over another, but God's glory can be seen better this way.

1.   **We Must be, Reconciled** -

Joseph looked past the fault and saw that he and his brothers needed to put their heads together. Doing this caused him to break down with many emotions. He fell on their necks and cried as he held them. The many bitter years they spent apart was suddenly within one minute made to vanish away.

When I read this portion of scripture, it began a wellspring of emotions bubbling up in my soul. The Holy Ghost immediately began to draw my attention to the parallel between this event and what must take place in the Body of Christ as we seek God's order. Joseph and his brothers weep together or acknowledged their wrongs against their brother and they begin the healing process as they wept and held each other. Reconciliation must begin by repentance.

Matthew 5:22-24 *"But I say unto you, That whosoever is angry with his brother without a cause shall be in danger of the judgment: and whosoever shall say to his brother, Raca, shall be in danger of the council: but whosoever shall say, Thou fool, shall be in danger of hell fire. 23. Therefore if thou bring thy gift to the altar, and there rememberest that thy brother hath ought against thee; 24. Leave there thy gift before the altar, and go thy way; first be reconciled to thy brother, and then come and offer thy gift."*

We must stop whatever we're doing at this hour in Christendom to reconcile with our brother or sister. How else will the work get done? We need our brother. What they have, we need, and what we have, they need.

Roman's 14: 10 *"But why doth thou judge thy brother? O why dost thou set at nought thy brother? For we shall all stand before the judgment seat of Christ."*

If we continue to judge them, we risk putting them at naught and, therefore, we can't be reconciled. But our means of mending what has been torn apart is to forgive.

James 5:16 *"But now ye rejoice in your boastings: all such rejoicing is evil."*

We need to sit down at some of our conferences and talk it out. We are sweeping the issues under the revival rug. We are in the same meeting places and no real union is taking place. You know how you just put up with someone, but you don't feel for them. I am not saying we will agree on everything, but I am saying we must be in agreement. This requires depth to our feelings for others regardless of what they have done to us. Healing can take place after we begin to care for our brothers and sisters in Christ, both personally and corporately.

1.   **Forgive Onesimus** -

Philemon 10-19 *"I beseech thee for my son Onesimus, whom I have begotten in my bonds: 11. Which in time past was to thee unprofitable, but now profitable to thee and to me. 12. Whom I have sent again: thou therefore receive him, that is, mine own bowels: 13. Whom I would have retained with me, that in thy stead he might have ministered unto me in the bonds of the gospel. 14. But without thy mind would I do nothing, that thy benefit should not be as it were of necessity, but willingly. 15. For perhaps he therefore departed for a season, that thou shouldest receive him for ever; 16. Not now as a servant, but above a servant, a brother beloved, specially to me, but how much more unto thee; both in the flesh and in the Lord? 17. If thou count me therefore a partner, receive him as myself. 18. If he has wronged thee, or oweth thee ought, put that on mine account.   19. I Paul have written it with mine own hand, I will repay it, albeit I do not say to thee how thou owest unto me even thine own self besides."*

Paul wrote to Philemon with a burdensome issue on his heart. He knew the tragedy of division among those in the Body. Onesimus was a servant to Philemon who had ran away at a great expense to Philemon. The Apostle Paul sought to initiate the reunion of the two by emphasizing the fact that they are brothers.

He told Philemon that maybe at one time he was of no value, but Onesimus is now profitable to you and to me. There are many situations like this in the Church from individuals, to pastors, to church affiliations, and to organizations. We must have a big heart to forgive "Onesimus' who is in our midst. It is our brotherly duty to strengthen the infirmities of the weak. Forgiveness will remove any animosity and allow us to come closer together in the gathering.

B.   **The Uprising -**

There is a group of people getting ready to be raised up by God so He can get the glory out of them. The castaways and those who aren't normally included or invited into what we consider holy settings are going to and are even now coming in droves to the Church. Others that are present in the Church will also rise along with the incoming souls. This will be called the"uprising," I know some people may be startled by this movement and even offended by what they perceive as a threat to their position or status in the Church. But this is another aspect of the gathering.

This immediately brings to my mind another uprising that shook up the aristocrats among the ecclesia in the Bible days. Jesus, Himself, was the leader of this revolt against the traditional religious party. He challenged them, not to cause controversy, but He sought change although it was controversial. This is the type of movement God is initiating in our midst.

It is consistent with His character for He oftentimes has chosen the last to make them first and demoted the first making them last. This is the uprising we are entrusted to discuss in this segment.

1.   **The Prodigal Son Is Coming Home -**

First, we must note that a prodigal is someone who has a radical personality. A prodigal goes after what he wants, because he is of the attitude "by any means necessary." He often is driven to acquire what is beyond his reach because he is a "go-getter", if you will.

In this familiar text, we see evidence of this younger son being a "go-getter" as he asks his father for his share in the inheritance. Many would criticize him for being this way, but we must look at the heart of the man. True, this attitude unrefined leads him to places and people that could not fulfill what was lacking in him. But, ultimately he was forced to acknowledge that his need was beyond what the pleasures of the world could provide. Be careful, for you could reject whom God accepts. Don't get caught up in who people are or what they have done or are doing. A thousand days are like one to God. He can change someone overnight or even in one minute elevating them to be who He always knew they would be. God sometimes does things undercover. He doesn't have to clue us in on any of His plans.

The Church can't be found in the posture and attitude of the elder brother who, incidentally, never left the father's house. But he was envious when his brother was celebrated for having come home. We must rejoice, as the angels do in heaven, at the coming home of any soul. Get ready because God is calling the prodigals home.

2.   **Go Get Jephthah!** -

Judges 11-1-8 *"Now Jephthah the Gileadite was a mighty man of valor, and he was the son of an harlot; and Gilead begat Jephthah. 2. And Gilead's wife bare him sons; and his wife's sons grew up, and they thrust out Jephthah and said unto him, Thou shalt not inherit in our father's house; for thou art the son of a strange woman. 3. Then Jephthah fled from his brethren, and dwelt in the land of Tob: and there were gathered vain men to Jephthah, and went out with him. 4. And it came to pass in process of time, that the children of Ammon made war against Israel. 5. And it was so, that when the children of Ammon made war against Israel, the elders of Gilead went to fetch Jephthah out of the land of Tob: 6. And they said unto Jephthah, Come, and be our captain, that we may fight with the children of Ammon. 7. And Jephthah said unto the elders of Gilead, did not ye hate me, and expel me out of my fathers's house? And why are ye come unto me now when ye are in distress? 8.And the elders of Gilead said unto Jephthah, Therefore we turn again to thee now, that thou mayest go with us, and fight against the children of Ammon, and be our head over all the inhabitants of Gilead."*

The Bible records many historical testimonies of various men and women throughout its pages. These people have a multiplicity of experiences, all of which involve an express move of God. The mystery, mercy and might of the Lord is revealed in each experience as He takes people from being the least, last and less likely to places, positions and piety never predicted of them. But God has a way that is mighty sweet. He will make the last first and the tail the head. He takes people like Ruth who, being a Moabitess woman, didn't have a legal right to the inheritance of Israel, yet He added her name in the will as an heir.

He will use people like David, who was the last son and was promoted to be king over a nation of God's people, contradicting both law and tradition. Esther, who was a hidden beauty in an ugly place, was brought out of obscurity in the kingdom for such as time as this to be a queen. The list goes on with Rahab, Jacob, Joseph and others in our era who are not written about in the Bible or any historical manuscript. As a matter of fact some of you are a paradigm of Jepthah.

We know God will do it for anybody, because Jephthah is a prime example illustrating for us how God will exalt the humble. Looking at the biblical record of his life, we see the basis for his humility. His mother was an adulterous harlot who had a child outside of the union of marriage. She was just a woman on the side for Jephthah's father. Her name seems to be to shameful to be mentioned by the text and further we don't read about her involvement in her son's life anywhere else in scripture. In light of being seemingly abandoned, somehow or another, despite this shady background, Jephthah was initially allowed in his father's house.

His brothers later openly confronted him with voices of disapproval about his background and went even as far as to say that he couldn't be a beneficiary of their father's inheritance. Things got so bad, they put their half brother out of their father's house. It reminded me of the story of Cinderella, and how her step sisters abused her and treated her like a second class citizen. I must make a point here, because this is related to the Church's order.

There are people in our midst who because they didn't get saved like we did, are being ostracized and excommunicated for being different. We do so just by having the attitude that we are better than they are. But all have sinned and come short of the glory of God. All our righteousness is as filthy rags. God always has sheep that are of another fold. God's choice is never subject to our approval. After all, isn't it the Father's house anyway. We are just the caretakers and laborers in it.

The "Jephthah's" are the persons who are dressed differently. Their hair may not be pinned up or nicely groomed. This kind may wear tattoos or pierce their bodies. Yet, we must validate them, so to not shut them out. If we don't receive them, where else will they go?

Jephthah in the text left [his home] and found himself sided with some worthless men who joined themselves to him. We are responsible for these people we have cast off, as if we are holier than they are.

a.   **God will use him -**

The next portion of the text deals with how God will allow the gift of those we have rejected to make room for them. As a matter of fact, God will force us to need them because their gift and talent are profitable to the Body. Look at the influence Jephthah had on these worthless men. Just think, if this influence was used to motivate people for God. We think we don't need him, but young people will look up to somebody they can identify with. They want to be able to look at a person and know that he or she has been through a similar situation and made it out alive. And if we tell the truth so do we. This is why these kinds of people's testimony is so impacting to other people's lives.

This leads us to the next topic of discussion, The word "Tob," which was the place Jephthah fled to, means "good." Check this out, Jephthah's brothers had expelled him from the father's house and, I guess they figured he wasn't important enough to be accepted. But look at the wisdom of God; He allowed Jephthah to be in a place called good that others didn't know about. It represents that God has some folk in a safe place or safe house, if you will, where He says, "I can still save them, although everybody else has concluded there is no hope." God specializes in this type of miraculous comeback. He will wait until people have said ashes to ashes and dust to dust and worms are crawling out of their dead carcasses. Then He'll say, "Lazarus, come forth"and make his critics take off his grave clothes. This is indicative of the way God moves mysteriously. Don't count anybody out, nothing is too hard for God nor anyone too difficult.

The brothers and the town's people are backed in a corner with no way out. Nobody has the skill or valor for the job of defending them against the enemy. They are forced to "go get Jephthah." This is getting good. God is calling us to "go get the Jephthah's", whoever they are or wherever they may be and whatever state they may be in. God wants to use a Jephthah in the last days, as we are going to the next level, the devil is, too. We need the Jephthah's to defeat the type of demons that are in the world today. We can't beat the giant with Saul's armor or sword. But we need a radical David type that doesn't care about protocol or tradition, but wants to knock out the devil with a sling shot and a rock and cut his head off. People are radical like that today. They believe in gang banging, drug dealing, gun slinging, lesbianism, homosexuality, bi-sexuality and, anything else that goes. Yet, out of these some what undesirable lifestyles are treasures hidden in trash.

John 3:16 *"God so loved the world that he gave his only begotten Son that whosoever will believe in Him shall have everlasting life."*

The emphasis must be put on **whosoever,** although they may be the very people you feel are not worthy of God. Church, "go get Jephthah." His or her name means "salvation" and they are in a place called Tob (good). In other words, they can be saved because God has preserved them for the express purpose of using them to His unequivocal glory. Isn't God awesome in His mercy and sovereignty which extends from eternity into time where we live.

Prayer: Father, in the Name of Jesus, I pray that you get our hearts right and please, Lord, begin to change our ways of thinking. In the Name of Jesus, God deal with our wrong attitudes toward people. Give us a mind set to be compassionate and receptive of all men and women no matter what their background or present status. Give us the compassion of Christ, that none would perish. Cause us to go after and to get the lost and the lonely. In the Name of Jesus, Lord forgive us, cleanse us from our previous state and renew in us a right spirit and create in us a clean heart. I thank you for the victory in advance. Amen.

C. **An Altar For A Nation -**

II. Chronicles 7:12-22(NKJV) *"Then the Lord appeared to Solomon by night, and said to him: "I have heard your prayer and have chosen this place for Myself as a house of sacrifice. 13. When I shout up heaven and there was no rain, or command the locust to devour the land, or send pestilence among My people, 14. If My people who are called by My name will humble themselves, and pray and seek My face, and turn from their wicked way, then I will hear from heaven, and I will forgive their sin and heal their land. 15. Now my eyes will open and My ears attentive to prayer made in this place. 16. For now I have chosen and sanctified this house, that My name may be there forever: and My eyes and My heart will be there perpetually. 17. As for you, if you walk before Me as your father David walked, and do according to all that I have commanded you, and if you keep My judgements, 18. Then I will establish the throne of your kingdom, as I covenanted with David your father, saying, "You shall not fail to have a man as a ruler in Israel." 19. "But if you turn away and forsake My commandments which I have set before you, and go and serve other gods, and worship them, 20. "then I will uproot them from My land which I have given them; and this house which I have sanctified for My name I will cast out of My sight, and will make it a proverb and a byword among all peoples. 21. And as for this house, which is exalted, everyone who passes by it will be astonished and say, Why has the Lord done thus to this land and this house?' 22. Then they will answer, 'Because they forsook the Lord God of their fathers, who brought them out of the land of Egypt, and embraced other gods, and worshiped. them and served them; therefore He has brought all this calamity on them."*

Once we all resume our positions we must assembly ourselves at the altar. God is calling a nation to an altar before Him. It's not a particular geographical location. It's a spiritual plateau where we are to be, so we can approach God as a unified chosen generation, a royal priesthood, and a holy nation who are His own special people that we may proclaim the praises of Him that called us out of darkness into the marvelous light.

The Church is being called to pray in the presence of her Master for the purpose of kindling an intimate relationship with Him. We won't come together in one central place, for there is no conference hall or super-dome large enough to contain the masses that make up the Body of Christ. We will be one when we together seek the One true and living God.

In the scriptures preceding II Chronicles chapter 7, all the way back to II Chron. chapter 5, we see the stage being set for our text. Solomon has completed the temple, has prayed the prayer of dedication, and the glory of God has filled the temple. That, by itself, is a point to be made. After the temple is built or the Church is in order, the glory of God will fall upon us and fill us.

The people of Israel, after witnessing this, fell with their faces to the pavement to worship God. Then at the completion of these events, God appeared to Solomon at night with a word that would prove to be what they needed to be revived. I believe their answer is also ours. The results of being out of order are that we will have no rain (no anointing). Locusts will devour our land - (our means of edification consumed by the devil); locusts and pestilence will be among the people - (we are left totally unable to function like God wills). The answer God gave Solomon was profound.

If we, His people, who carry His name, can humble ourselves (be real) and pray (with our whole heart), seek His face, which means we will have to make a U-turn from our wicked ways, then God will hear us, forgive us, and heal us, and our land. We need to form an altar for our nation.

Looking back in this Chapter at the 12th verse, we can hear something God says to help us go forward to our next discussion. He says to Solomon, in II Chronicles 7:12, I have heard thy prayer, and have chosen this place to myself for a house of sacrifice. Let's talk about this for a moment.

1.   **Sacrifice -**

Genesis 22:1-17 *"And it came to pass after these things, that God did tempt Abraham, and said unto him, Abraham: and he said, Behold, here I am. 2. And he said, Take now they son, thine only son Isaac, whom thou lovest, and get thee into the land of Moriah; and offer him there for a burnt offering upon one of the mountains which I will tell thee of. 3. And Abraham rose up early in the morning, and saddled his ass, and took two of his young men with him, and Isaac his son, and clave the wood for the burnt offering, and rose up, and went unto the place of which God had told him. 4. Then on the third day Abraham lifted up his eyes, and saw the place afar off. 5. And Abraham said unto his young men, Abide ye here with the ass; and I and the lad will go yonder and worship, and come again to you. 6. And Abraham took the wood of the brunt offering, and laid it upon Isaac his son; and he took the fire in his hand, and a knife; and they went both of them together. 7. and Isaac spake unto Abraham his father, and said, my father; and he said, Here am I, my son. And he said, Behold the fire and the wood: But where is the lamb for a burnt offering? 8. And Abraham said, My son, God will provide himself a lamb for a burnt offering: so they went both of them together. 9. And they came to the place which God had told him of; and Abraham built an altar there, and laid the wood in order, and bound Isaac his son, and laid him on the altar upon the wood. 10. And Abraham stretched forth his hand, and took the knife to slay his son. 11. and the angel of the LORD called unto him out of heaven, and said, Abraham, Abraham: and he said, Here am I. 12. And he said, Lay not thine hand upon the lad, neither do thou any thing unto him; for now I know that thou fearest God, seeing thou hast not withheld thy son, thine only son from me. 13. And Abraham lifted up his eyes, and looked, and behold behind him a ram caught in a thicket by his horns; and Abraham went and took the ram, and offered him up for a burnt offering in the stead of his son. 14. And Abraham called the name of the place Jehovah jireh: as it is said to this day, In the mount of the LORD it shall be seen. 15. And the angel of the LORD called unto Abraham out of heaven the second time, 16. And said, By myself have I sworn, saith the Lord, for because thou hast done this thing, and has not withheld thy son, thine only son: 17. That in blessing I will bless thee, and in multiplying I will multiply thy seed as the stars of the heaven, and as the sand which is upon the sea shore; and thy seed shall possess the gate of his enemies."*

After we get to the altar as a nation, we must sacrifice to our God. Christian vernacular is colored with the frequent use of the word sacrifice. As a matter of fact, it is so redundantly spoken, we have almost become deaf to its meaning, which speaks of devotion, consecration, and veneration causing us to go to every extreme to commit to God. Therefore, I believe that if we are to do any justice to this discussion, we must first unveil the hidden wealth we have buried beneath the phonics and writing of the word.

As to the literal meaning, the English dictionary says sacrifice is an offering of a life, whether animal, plant or human. It can also be one of an inanimate material possession. The mentality of the one making the sacrifice must be one of surrendering or destroying something as a prize or something most desirable for the sake of something else that is considered as having a higher or more pressing claim.

Going higher, we must scale the wall for knowledge to further overlook this word which has four distinct Hebrew meanings describing a few variations of the word "sacrifice." The first word is quōban. It means "brought near", an offering as a symbol of communication or covenant between man and God. Secondly, there is the word mĭnhäh. It means something given; a gift or tribute (a bloodless offering). Thirdly, the word zëbäh; which means to slay; bloody sacrifice. Finally, Óälah, which means whole burnt offering; to give whole to sacrifice completely burning. The Greek language has one word usage for sacrifice which is Thusia. This word embodies all the sacrifices that one can make.

The history of sacrificial acts can be traced back as far as when man first needed reconciliation for his sin in the Garden of Eden. It was given as an example by God to Adam and his wife. He took the skin of an animal, meaning that an animal had to die, and placed it for a covering over Adam and Eve's nakedness.

These acts would continue to be performed by Cain and Abel, Noah and Abraham, and from Abraham to Moses and from Moses to Jesus. Now it is through and by Jesus that we have access and the means of making a more excellent sacrifice due to the ultimate blood sacrifice He made. Therefore, we by believing in Him can take part in the act of sacrifice.

There is a song we sing in my church that says, "We don't have to slay the lamb anymore, we don't have to put no more blood on the door. Someone has taken the place of the lamb, His name is Jesus, the Great I Am." It rings true–we don't have to offer bulls, sheep (lamb), goats, doves, pigeons, or cooked grain mixed with oil anymore.

The preceding text records for us the events surrounding the sacrifice God required of Abraham. We read that he heard God calling him to sacrifice the son He had promised him, which was the son Abraham had loved so much. It was understandable because he had waited for his birth so long. Certainly it would be expected of him to become close to his son in every possible way.

As did Abraham, God is calling the Church to sacrifice what we love so much. Anything that has been allowed to climb to the top of our pedestals taking the place of God must be sacrificed. It slowly, yet surely, has caused us to yield our focus on other things, places, and people. There is a gradual process taking place, syphoning away at the attention that we normally would completely be giving to the Lord. With utter urgency we must expose and expel this enemy to our relationship with our God.

Looking back at the record, this didn't just happen, Abraham had started to concentrate on the promise, Isaac, more than God who promised, prior to our immediate text. In Genesis 15:2-4 Abraham asked God to make his servant's son heir to the promise and he later tried to use Haggar as a means of helping to birth the promise. We see the connotation of how Abraham shifts his attention to what God promised, rather than keeping it on the Lord. The world would argue, that if God gave me this, shouldn't I love it or them. Isn't my own flesh and blood just as important? True enough, we are suppose to love what God gives us, but the balance is that we love it or them through Him so He can filter out any impurities. The danger in loving something or someone more than the Lord is that this level of devotion easily escalates to the act of worship. If we worship anything, it will demand we sacrifice to it. To do that defies the commandment of God against performing acts of sacrifice to idols. God is a jealous God and He demands worship to Him only.

To better understand the danger and seriousness of worshiping anything other than God, we must again do a word study. The word worship must be better defined for our purposes in this discourse. Worship means worthy or more at worth. In other words, worth more. When something or someone is worshiped, you are saying that they are worth more than all else including God. You know this has become true when it gets most of our attention, time, and money. Almost every thought begins, ends, or reflects in some way about it. Don't let anything be worth more than God in your life. Church, we are being called to worship God, and Him only in spirit and in truth to the extent we will sacrifice all and any for Him.

Back to the text, we read that God tells Abraham further to go to the land of Moriah to sacrifice. Moriah was a hill above where Abraham was. It means, to see or gaze upon the Lord most vehemently. God is beckoning us to go to a higher place, away from our normal environment expressly for the purpose of making the ultimate sacrifice to Him.

When I was studying the geographical location of the events surrounding the text, I found it noteworthy that the distance Abraham traveled to get to Moriah was about fifty miles. This fact alone makes known to us that it won't be easy to sacrifice. During his trek toward devotion, Abraham had all the needed tools handy. One of the things the text says he had struck me as strange. It said he had fire in his hand for an undetermined length of time during his journey. Fire can and is often used to denote the word desire or the burning sensation that is associated with it. It was this fire that lit this worshipers's path on the way up the hilltop where he would further use it to finalize his ultimate act of sacrifice.

As Abraham finds his way, the climax of the moment reaches its peak and it is in this atmosphere that this man of God builds an altar for his sacrifice. If we will sacrifice what separates our souls from our Savior, we must build an altar for what we must sacrifice. Prayer sets the platform for what must die. It causes a person to focus on God and de-emphasize everything and everyone else. Prayer is a means of fortifying us from the isolation of sin to insulate us with God's righteousness. We must build our altar; it might require blood, sweat and many tears, but this is the fundamental stage that must precede our final act of worship. Where else will we get the strength to let go of what we like holding onto and make what has a hold of us let go.

We must place our sacrifice on our altar so it will die. That altar isn't located in the church building itself or on a stone or rock, but its location is in our heart. David said he wanted to hide the word in his heart so that he wouldn't sin against God. Abraham also brought a knife to aid him in killing what was to be sacrificed. The word is described in scripture as a two-edged sword. We need the word of God to kill what is trying to divide us from our God.

This may seem easy enough, but this can be difficult, because when something dies that is so connected to you, even down to our DNA, it hurts. Some of our reasons for not going ahead and sacrificing is that it hurts to let go of what we love. Those of us who boast that we quit this and stopped that, can't really brag, because if it was that easy those weren't true sacrifices. You really sacrifice something or someone when it hurts down in your belly to let it or them go. This is the dilemma Abraham was faced with, for the sacrifice was his son that God had long promised him.

If I may digress, before Jesus was to sacrifice Himself, He struggled with the idea of what He would suffer in the cup from which He had to drink. We read that this experience caused Him much grief. As He prayed, drops of sweat from His brow produced blood. Like Jesus, Abraham pressed on, regardless, and as a result God showed up with provisions. What was so painful became joyful. God had never intended to take what He had given him, He only wanted to purify Abraham's motives for wanting what He gave him.

God is going to provide what we need supernaturally to do what has to be done; but we, as the Church, must commence to sacrificing. Thus, becoming in the last days sold out for the Lord with our whole hearts. Paul highlights this idea as a Christian theme in II Corinthians 4:7-12.

"But we have this treasure in earthen vessels, that the excellency of the power may be of God, and not of us. 8. We are troubled on every side, yet not distressed; we are perplexed, but not in despair; 9. Persecuted, but not forsaken; cast down, but not destroyed; 10. Always bearing about in the body the dying of the Lord Jesus, that the life also of Jesus might be made manifest in our body. 11. For we which live are always delivered unto death for Jesus' sake, that the life also of Jesus might be made manifest in our mortal flesh. 12. So then death worketh in us, but life in you. **And I Corinthians 15:30-31 -** *And why stand we in jeopardy every hour? 31. I protest by your rejoicing which I have in Christ Jesus our Lord, I die daily."*

We must die daily, laying anything and everyone we love more than God on the altar of our heart to be sacrificed as we heed God's command.

PRAYER: Help God. We find it hard to lay before you the things and people we have become accustomed to and even love dearly. Yet God, we acknowledge these are the very obstacles to our relationship with you. <u>Give us strength to go through with the sacrifice</u>. Give us what we need to commit our all to you. It is in Jesus' Name we pray. Let us leave it or them there until we are crucified to it and it is to us. Amen.

2.　　**Built on Tears -**

Our nation has an altar and it is there we must at this time weep before our God. These tears make-up our bricks, cinder blocks, steel beams, and drywall we will have to use to reorganize the Church that we are rebuilding. The tears prepare the place where we must establish the foundation. They soften the hard places that have retarded our ability to go forth with the construction of the edifice. This is where the tabernacle for God's glory will stand.

a.   **David cried -**

II Samuel 24:18-25 *"And Gad came that day to David, and said unto him, Go up, rear an altar unto the LORD, in the threshing floor of Araunah the Jebusite. 19. And David, according to the saying of Gad, went up as the LORD commanded. 20. And Araunah looked, and saw the king and his servants coming on toward him; and Araunah went out, and bowed himself before the king on his face upon the ground. 21. And Araunah said, Wherefore is my lord the king come to his servant? And David said, To buy the threshing floor of thee, to build an altar unto the LORD, that the plague may be stayed from the people. 22. And Araunah said unto David, Let my lord the king take and offer up what seemeth good unto him: behold, here be oxen for burnt sacrifice, and threshing instruments and other instruments of the oxen for wood. 23. All these things did Araunah, as a king, give unto the king. And Araunah said unto the king, The LORD thy God accept thee. 24. And the king said unto Araunah, Nay: but I will surely buy it of thee at a price: neither will I offer burnt offerings unto the LORD my God of that which doth cost me nothing. So David bought the threshingfloor and the oxen for fifty shekels of silver. 25. And David built there an altar unto the LORD, and offered burnt offerings and peace offerings. So the LORD was entreated for the land, and the plague was stayed from Israel."*

David was characterized as a man after God's own heart. It is he who is responsible for the majority of the Psalms written. The Psalms are filled with endearing words from this king's heart as he sought God continuously through praise and worship. David, in the text, was faced with a detrimental dilemma. He had to make amends for putting confidence in the number of people God had given him to lead, as well as preventing these people from giving the required offering at the time of census. I believe God dealt so forcefully with this offence because it opened the door for David to worship the blessing more that the giver of the blessing. God is a jealous God when it comes to the worship He should receive from His people. He demands that no other god be worshiped other than Him.

The challenge was now on; David had resolved to repent and make the sacrifice to his God, that He demanded he make. As a matter of fact, he was so adamant about it that even though Araunah the Jebusite offered out of respect for his position to give all he needed to make the sacrifice, including the threshing floor, he declined with the words, *"No, but I will surely buy it from you for a price; nor will I offer burnt offerings to the Lord my God with that which costs me nothing."* There is a painful price to be paid if we are going to re-establish right relationship with God. Believe me when I say to you nothing is worth having that's free, and no pain–no gain. We as a Church must dispel the myth of this bowl of cherries and cream puff type of theology. We must know it will cost us a lot and often, if not all of the time, and with many tears as David writes in Psalm 43:3, *"My tears have been my meat day and night, while they continually say unto me, Where is thy God?"*

Jesus also wept in the Garden of Gethsemane prior to His ultimate sacrifice. His sacrifice was able to be made because His altar had been anointed with tears. He, too, decided to pay the cost with words that echo David's actions *"Nevertheless, thy will be done,"* in other words, I'll pay the cost.

This place had been visited once before by the patriarch Abraham. The aroma of sacrifice was already in the air from ages prior to this occasion. The hill called Moriah again set the tone for what was yet to come in the very same place.

b.   **Solomon Built -**

Nothing can proceed forward as to the order of the Church or the building of God's temple of glory until we have paid the price. David left the plans and pattern for the temple to Solomon. He built it on that familiar site of sacrifice that Abraham used and David his father purchased at a cost to use. Moriah would be the place for the grand finale of sacrifices made before now. This hill would continue to be a perpetual place of sacrifice. The tears lie underneath the foundation and atop of them is the glory of the Lord.

After Solomon completed the construction of this sacred edifice, he dedicated this holy temple to God with prayer. All the work was done and now it was time that the temple be occupied by its resident and owner.

II Chronicles 7:1-3 *"Now when Solomon had made an end of praying, the fire came down from heaven, and consumed the burnt offering and the sacrifices; and the glory of the LORD filled the house. 2. And the priests could not enter into the house of the LORD, because the glory of the LORD had filled the LORD's HOUSE. 3. And when all the children of Israel saw how the fire came down, and the glory of the LORD upon the house, they bowed themselves with their faces to the ground upon the pavement, and worshiped, and praised the LORD, saying, For he is good; for his mercy endureth forever."*

The temple was not erected abstractly, but with purpose. It represents the Church as being in order, and it is a direct result of us corporately kneeling before an altar before our God. Then, the Holy Ghost filled the temple. We are the temple for God's presence to reside. This kind of atmosphere will make it difficult for the preachers to preach, and those that praise to praise, as it did the priest who couldn't go into the temple to minister. This is when God does it all. He will send his glory to fill the house and the purifying fire from heaven will sanctify us who are the house of God.

D.   **The Outpouring -**

Psalm 133:1-3 *"Behold, how good and how pleasant it is for brethren to dwell together in unity! 2. It is like the precious ointment upon the head, that ran down upon the beard, even Aaron's beard; that went down to the skirts of his garments; 3. As the dew of Hermon, and as the dew that descended upon the mountains of Zion; for there the LORD commanded the blessing, even life for evermore."* Joel 2:28-32 *"And it shall come to pass afterward, that I will pour out my spirit upon all flesh; and your sons and your daughters shall prophesy, your old men shall dream dreams, your young men shall see visions; 29. And also upon the servants and upon the handmaids in those days will I pour out my spirit. 30. And I will shew wonders in the heavens and in the earth, blood, and fire, and pillars of smoke. 31. The sun shall be turned into darkness, and the moon into blood, before the great and terrible day of the LORD come. 32. And it shall come to pass, that whosoever shall call on the name of the LORD shall be delivered: for in mount Zion and in Jerusalem shall be deliverance, as the LORD hath said, and in the remnant whom the LORD shall cast."* Acts 2:1-4 *"And when the day of Pentecost was fully come, they were all with one accord in one place. 2. And suddenly there came a sound from heaven as of a rushing mighty wind, and it filled all the house where they were sitting. 3. And there appeared unto them cloven tongues like as of fire, and it sat upon each of them. 4. And they were all filled with the Holy Ghost, and began to speak with other tongues, as the Spirit gave them utterance."*

There is power in our being unified in one place and on one accord. The text in Psalms allows us to take a glimpse at the concept and results of us coming together. The ointment or anointing runs down from our High Priest, Christ, meaning the anointed one, and flows to the Body of Christ, Zion. This precious oil is the means by which we can be the witnesses for Jesus in this world.

Jesus said so in the first chapter of Acts, telling His disciples that they would receive power after that the Holy Ghost came upon them, then they would be His witnesses in Jerusalem, Judea, Samaria and the uttermost parts of the world. The paramount reason we as a Church must get *in order* is that the oil won't run in a full flow out of the horn of heaven above us, until we get in one place with one focus in the same Spirit. It will be like the oil which only poured upon David (a type of Christ) once he stood in the right place. We need the oil or anointing to do what God has ordained us to do. But we must get in place under our head, Christ Jesus who is our High priest.

1. **Grace Before Greatness** -

Ephesians 1:1-9 *"Paul, an apostle of Jesus Christ by the will of God, to the saints which are at Ephesus, and to the faithful in Christ Jesus. 2. Grace be to you, and peace, from God our Father, and from the Lord Jesus Christ. 3. Blessed be the God and Father of our Lord Jesus Christ, who hath blessed us with all spiritual* *blessings in heavenly places in Christ: 4. According as he hath chosen us in him before the foundation of the world, that we should be holy and without blame before him in love: 5. Having predestinated us unto the adoption of children by Jesus Christ to himself, according to the good pleasure of his will, 6. To the praise of the glory of his grace, wherein he hath made us accepted in the beloved. <u>7. In whom we have</u> <u>redemption through his blood, the forgiveness of sins, according to the riches of his grace; 8. Wherein he hath abounded toward us in all wisdom and prudence;</u> 9. Having made known unto us the mystery of his will, according to his good pleasure which he hath purposed in himself:"* Ephesians 4:7 - *"But unto every one of us is given grace according to the measure of the gift of God."*

The book written to the Ephesians was authored by the Apostle Paul. He starts this particular manuscript or letter as he does all of his writings, in a similar way. <u>*"Grace to you and peace from our Father and the Lord Jesus Christ."*</u> In this letter, he mentions the word grace some twelve times and then ends with the closing statement: *"Grace be with all those who love our Lord Jesus Christ in sincerity, amen."*

The word grace as we obviously read, becomes a sort of signature literary trait of Paul. He mentions the word grace for a grand total of eighty-nine times throughout all of his writings. Every book he wrote is colored with the artistry of its letters and graphic meaning. This being true, it's not hard to conclude Paul our renowned author thought grace to be imperative for everybody to experience in its fullness.

Acts chapter 1:7 (NKJV) says: *"In Him [Jesus] we have redemption through His blood, the forgiveness of sins, according to the riches of His grace."*

This initial portion of the above text deals with an element of grace that is elementary in the whole process of grace. It expresses how salvation is a benefit of grace. Paul, along with other writers, said how it's only by grace through faith we are saved. But, he seals something more within this word as he envelopes a manifold treasure by using the word "riches" as a deeper description of grace. By implication, Paul leads us to understand that there is more grace than the grace there is for salvation.

I feel a lot of Christians miss out on the wealth that is embedded beneath the surface of this so commonly used word. Theologians have just about worn out the ink used to write this word. What we need to know is that saving grace is only the initial experience of grace for Christians. In its abundance, grace overflows over to another level and ultimately manifests our purpose in God's plan. Just like faith moves to faith and glory shuttles us to more glory, so does grace flow like a stream into a river and ends up into the ocean. Grace then transports us into and through another phase called suffering.

Verse eight of our text further alludes to grace beyond salvation, when it says, *"Which He, (Christ) made to abound toward us in all wisdom and prudence."* I can imagine that Paul was speaking here not just to lecture the readers, but he was testifying to his personal experiences. Paul could have brought up his first exposure to this grace as he had encountered it on the road to Damascus. It was here God looked beyond his misdeeds of persecuting the Church and saw he needed salvation.

He could go further and note the time he was stricken with a thorn in his flesh and had to pray three times without deliverance. His only consolation was through a word he received from God, *"His grace was sufficient enough to sustain him during his suffering(paraphrase)."* He received a revelation from God at this time that there is grace for suffering. Now it is this aspect of grace that sets the platform for our plateau. It is the area where Christians are made or broken. Crushing must take place at this stage like the olive is forced to undergo traumatic, external pressure that reveals its internal values. The oil is the treasured result of it having undergone this process of crushing.

Likewise, the Bride of Christ, the Church, must develop the persistence and attitude of the woman worshiper who pressed her way into the presence of her Lord Jesus Christ who had delivered and forgiven her from much. She persevered past the seated fixtures of faith who had been in Jesus' presence so long they lost their concern and need to care for Him. But strangely they envied her as she carelessly disregarded their high positions. They themselves nonchalantly sat in the room. But she had fixed her eyes on her familiar friend who redeemed her from all. In the hype of the moment, she lost the couth she never had anyway and sacrificed all she had locked within an alabaster box. Determined not to allow it to hinder her devotion, she broke it with reverent fervor, releasing the aromatic fragrance it contained. What she probably earned through her sexual improprieties would be exchanged for what was worth more to her. The ointment or oil came at a great cost, but surely it was nothing in comparison to having Jesus her Lord.

If we will experience the grace for suffering, we must be willing to break and be broken before Jesus. The box wasn't just an inanimate object in her hand, but it was representative a very animated life which had caused her to treasure it so dearly.

We, too, must allow ourselves to be crushed so the oil (grace) can be unleashed to mend, strengthen and fortify us for the next level of grace. Now please get this part. The simultaneous result of our being broken is that the room was left changed by this women's humble display of worship. The aroma of her testimony filled the meeting place and everybody coming in after her experienced the sweetness of her victory. It is the treasure within her that was unearthed to bring God glory.

The flesh and its natural propensities must be made humble so no flesh can glory in God's presence. It is the flesh which is the retaining wall holding back the oil stored up for us, and when it is crushed or broken down, the oil will freely flow like rivers refreshing our souls. This oil represents grace which is released during our suffering. It sustains us during the suspenseful issues of our lives. Thus grace continues to flow beyond suffering to and for service.

Paul in I Corinthians' 2:4 explains how God gives grace for service. This is our final phase of grace God is trying to take us to for this latter-day harvest.

I Corinthians 2:4 *"And my speech and my preaching was not with enticing words of man's wisdom, but in demonstration of the Spirit of power."*

The oil is not just used to minister healing during suffering, but it is also used many times in scripture to anoint men and women setting them apart for service. God's servant David said after having gone through the valley of the shadow of death, *"my cup runneth over."* If God has filled us with grace (oil) and it runs over, it is not to be wasted, but we are *blessed to be a blessing*. Church, we are moving fast toward this last stage of grace which is for service. The grace (anointing) will enable us to do what our Lord commands. It doesn't come without responsibility, for to whom much is given, much will be required.

a. **Service or Stardom -**

As we approach the dispensation of this era of service, we must assess our reasons for doing what we do. Because, although we are invested with the enabling power of the Holy Ghost, it can be abated by our wrong intentions. Let's look at some areas of intent.

Why do you do what you do? Is it for the glitter? Do we want to shine in the eyes of others for the purpose of being the "star" of our own show? Is it our name we desire to see in lights or are we hunting down cameras just to be caught on film? Do we seek the glamour of the moment? Is it the intoxicating euphoric effect we pursue? Do we want the power to enchant men or women to become, the object they worship? I hope not, please don't abase yourself to a cheap sex symbol or spiritual symbol, if you will. Finally, do we do what we do because of the glory? Have we gone over the absolute edge with our self-promoting? Have we, somehow, with great deception, thought the credit belongs to us?

Beware glory seekers! The glory belongs to God. There is no flesh He will allow to glory in His presence. God will knock over Dagon until he breaks before His presence. Remember, it is only by God's grace we can do anything that we do. Grace speaks to reserving all glory and spotlights for Jesus. He is the star of all shows and He says we don't have to be stars to be in His show.

1.   **Judah First -**

With these prior thoughts in mind, let us look at some events taking place in our present era. Judah means worship or praise; to revere or respect God. This is representative of the musical remnant God is sending ahead of the rest of the Body to set the stage. The tribe of Judah has to be mindful of their position. God wants and is using them as an advance to conquer the enemy. What I mean by this is that God is giving Judah the televised spotlight so the Priest and Levites can follow with the ark of the covenant containing the tablet of testimony (the word) and the presence of God. Judah who is responsible for leading worship, praise and singing in the Church and before the world must not choose stardom over service. You are duly appointed in the kingdom for such a time as this. As God opens the doors for the musically anointed, they must remain sober and stand for the standards of God in all that they are charged to sing and play. Don't stagger at what the world offers you. It's a trick that will lead to a trap. The price you will pay is losing your anointing. Then you'll be left standing on stages in an empty auditorium where there is no presence of God, just another cast away whose name is no longer at the top of the people's charts.

b.   **Blessed to be a Blessing -**

God called us to be servants instead of being served. All that He has given us wasn't meant to be hoarded by us, but to be a means of blessing someone else.

Genesis 12:2-3 *"And I will make of thee a great nation, and I will bless thee, and make thy name great; and thou shalt be a blessing; 3. And I will bless them that bless thee and curse him that curseth thee; and in thee shall all families of the earth be blessed."*

God's reason for blessing Abraham was not only because of him, but it also was meant to be a benefit to the whole earth. Jesus said to us *"ye are the light of the world and the salt of the earth."* We are blessed to be a blessing.

Acts 5:12-16 *"And by the hands of the apostles were many signs and wonders wrought among the people; (and they were all with one accord in Solomon's porch. 13. And of the rest durst no man join himself to them; but the people magnified them. 14. And believers were the more added to the Lord, multitudes both of men and women.) 15. <u>Insomuch that they brought forth the sick into the streets, and laid them on beds and couches, that at the least the shadow of Peter passing by might overshadow some of them.</u> 16. There came also a multitude out of the cities round about unto Jerusalem, bringing sick folks, and them which were vexed with unclean spirits; and they were healed everyone."*

Peter for example was blessed by the power of God to the personal benefit of his own life. He walked in the light of the Lord and yet he walked among those in need of a blessing. As a result of being blessed and being in a place to bless, his shadow which was only a result of the Light (Jesus), healed and ministered to others in need.

The Church must get in the light of Jesus and as we walk therein, let us go to those in need. Surely then many will be blessed by us. Lives will be changed as souls are saved and revival breaks out in the world due to the benevolence of the Body of Christ through C   h   r   i   s   t   J   e   s   u   s   .

The order of God is to re-establish a different Spirit in this world. He has chosen His Church to manifest the power of God into peoples situations. So they will know there is hope in the midst of chaos.

Judgment must begin first in the household of faith. For it is then we can go forth and display God's glory and rightly show forth the praises of our Lord. Go ye therefore now that you know you have the power after that the Holy Ghost has come upon you.

We need to look at one last story in the Bible that can aid us in understanding this point of being a servant more than one who is served. The prodical son for instance went home with a changed perspective on being a servant. Having suffered during his wild escapades, the prodical son learned that being blessed came with responsibility. Returning home he resolved to do more than seek his inheritance as before, but he sought to serve this time. Like King David, he had the testimony that he would rather be a doorman as long as he could be in God's house. The power behind this statement is almost to awesome to get. The king was saying that he had to serve. The prodical son was changing his "give me, give me" attitude to one of being satisfied to just serve. This is what positioned him to get the robe and ring to celebrate his welcomed return home. God wants the Church to get the character of the servant. Then we will be in true fellowship with Him and each other. Jesus said to the disciples who were arguing who would be the greatest in Mark 9:35 *"if any man desires to be first, the same shall be last of all and servant of all."* Later in Luke 22;27 Jesus addresses this same issue by saying *" but I am among you as he that serveth".* In other words, as He was sent, we are blessed to be a blessing.

Let's pray: Father in the name of Jesus, I ask that you bind our bless me, bless me, attitude that we've had, and open our bowels of compassion. Help us to be available for your purpose to a world in need of our light and salt that you have entrusted to the Church. Father, it is in the Name of Jesus I thank you. Hallelujah, be glory to God Most High. Bless the Lord from whom all blessings flow.

Thank you, God, for Your grace that not only saved us but also has brought us to this dispensation in time for the purpose unto which you have called us as your Church from the beginning. Now God, move upon your people wherever they are physically and spiritually. Cause them, God, to get in order with your will, so that we can hasten toward our destiny in you. Fall, Holy Ghost, rise in the people of God. Stir up the gifts and anoint them to serve until they bless this world to see light in our works, so they will be free to glorify You and be saved just the same. In Jesus' Name , I pray that the yoke of confusion and disorder will be destroyed. I pray that healing will yield reconciliation. Reveal to your people what is their place and calling in your will Father. I ask all these prayers in Jesus' Name. Amen!

Now praise God with me Saints, lift up the name of Jesus. Go ahead that's right, exalt Him until heaven comes down with power and hell is scattered. Praise our Savior until He is lifted and men and women are drawn unto Him. Thank you Lord for your work through your Church in advance. Glory to you Jesus, our soon coming King, you are worthy, most high God.

Benediction:

For now this is the end of the matter at hand. God has used me and now He wants to use you. We are to be collectively harnessed by the power of the Holy Ghost as an instrument of salvation, deliverance, healing, help and hope to a world that will be destitute without our God. The challenge has been administered to all that read and would hear the Spirit of God speaking to their innate spirit. I feel the move of God churning in the atmosphere like a cloud above our heads ready to down pour an abundance of rain upon the waiting assembly of saints. The masses who are rejuvenated by our Father will be those that launch out into the deep of darkness to walk on the unbelievable as they hear a familiar voice saying *"come."* It will be our attempt that pleases our Master as He takes our hand bringing us back together in our vessel (mode of movement). As the Lord carries us to a safe and orderly place therein, He will silence the chaos of the storm. Bless you, my family of believers forever and forever, peace and grace be unto you.

If you were blessed and inspired by this message and would either like to purchase more copies of this book or contact the author for any speaking engagements for any meeting or occasion, call :

call # 301-209-0089

e-mail <u>arronwill@yahoo.com</u>

Mail to Evangelist Arron D. Williams c/o, <u>Greater Mt. Calvary Holy Church/ 610 Rhode Island ave NE Washington, D.C. 20002</u>